THE COLORFUL WORLD OF THE CIRCUS

OPEN DAILY
BOOK HERE! BOOK HERE!
CIRCUS ADVANCE BOOKING
BOOK HERE
BOOK HERE
BOOK HERE

THE COLORFUL WORLD OF THE CIRCUS

DAVID JAMIESON
SANDY DAVIDSON

FOREWORD BY
HELEN WALLENDA

OCTOPUS

CONTENTS

Page 1
Sonny Fossett, chief clown of Gerry Cottle's Circus.

Pages 2 and 3
*The 1976 Circus World Championships, Big Top,
Clapham Common, London.*

Left
Louis Knie's tigers, Circus Knie, Switzerland.

First Published 1980 by
Octopus Books Limited
59 Grosvenor Street
London W1

ISBN 0 7064 0694 1

© 1980 Octopus Books Limited

Produced by Mandarin Publishers Limited
22a Westlands Road
Quarry Bay, Hong Kong

Printed in Hong Kong

FOREWORD

Several generations of my own family and that of my husband have had the circus in their blood – we ourselves were performers for over sixty years. And it seems to me that *The Love of the Circus* reflects the true life of the Circus which we loved – the romance and the razzle-dazzle is complemented by the hard work behind the scenes and the business management.

David Jamieson and Sandy Davidson present today's circus in all its forms throughout the world. The circus's outstanding acts are discussed in detail and pictured in exciting colour photographs which capture the glamour and excitement which make up its charm.

The Love of the Circus is a book I very much enjoyed reading and I am sure that everyone who picks it up will be enthralled from cover to cover.

Helen Wallenda

HELEN WALLENDA

Left: *Mary Chipperfield and her beautiful Andalusian High School horse, Pedro.*

THE CIRCUS ON PARADE

What is the circus? The circus is a unique combination of ingredients which can appeal to anyone, regardless of race, creed or education. The circus is international, crossing all barriers since its success is not dependent on language. It is visual, sensual and basic. There can be few countries in the world which today do not have their own circuses or visits from ones from elsewhere.

Although superficially there are links between the circus now and the circuses of ancient Rome, the aims of the two are directly opposite. The most successful attractions of the Roman amphitheatres were violent and bloody struggles, often to the death – the gladiators, the chariot races and the ghastly slaughter of wild animals. The whole essence of the modern circus is of men and animals working in harmony together. Only through close teamwork can the flying trapeze artistes successfully achieve the triple somersault or the tiger trainer produce impressive routines which display the natural beauty of his big cats.

Left: *In America, most circuses have three rings, with three acts performing simultaneously, and the most celebrated of them all is the Ringling Brothers and Barnum & Bailey 'Combined Show', seen here in New York's Madison Square Garden. With over 200 performers, 100 animals and a plethora of props and rigging, the staging of 'The Greatest Show on Earth' demands the highest degree of organizational skill.*

In fact, the modern circus has its origins in London in the late eighteenth century when acrobats, tumblers and a clown were added to displays of trick riding. As the entertainment became more successful, it moved into its own special buildings and, later, into tents. The circus spread from England to Europe and subsequently throughout the globe. During the nineteenth century, wild animals came into the circus; various new forms of acrobatic displays were introduced; and, in 1859, the most romantic and athletic of all the circus skills was seen for the first time – the flying trapeze.

Today, the type of acts that you see in the world's circuses – whether it's Ringling Brothers (with its two units – the Red and the Blue) in America or Chipperfields in Britain or Ashtons in Australia or Circus Krone in Germany or the Cirque Bouglione in France – will essentially be the same as those which entertained audiences during the last century. Of course, each country has given the circus its own special character. The Americans traditionally require their circuses to have three rings. They look for size and spectacle and a multitude of performers and animals as much as the talents of individual acts. The European circuses, however, almost always feature one ring and derive much of their appeal from the close proximity of spectator and artiste so that the audience can become much more involved in what is going on in the ring. In Eastern European countries, the circus is run by the state and has been given the status of an art form. Good training facilities have helped the State Circuses of Bulgaria, Hungary, Romania, East Germany and, above all, Russia to raise the standard of acrobatics in the circus to an impressively high level. Further east, acrobatics are ubiquitous in the shows put on in Taiwan, China and Korea and these companies, which have been seen in the west on several recent occasions, bring a delightful grace and power to their work which is quite unlike the less subtle presentation of western circuses.

Right: *The travelling circus is a unique community, spending a few weeks or days at each location – in effect, a town within a town. This is the Robert Brothers' Circus, one of Britain's biggest, at Greenock in Scotland. The lay-out is basically the same on every site. The menagerie is on the left of the big top, with canvas stables for the elephants, horses, ponies and camels and mobile cages for the lions and tigers. The circus has its own electricity generators, fire engine, refuse waggon and toilets. On the right of the big top are the giant articulated living waggons of the Robert Brothers' families. The whole show can be transported from one town to another in under 24 hours.*

Left: *The late nineteenth century was the Golden Age of Circus. A magnificent free publicity parade would be held on arrival in a new town. All the artistes and staff and the elephants, horses and camels would take part and there were superb tableau waggons. This one, restored by the Circus World Museum in Baraboo, Wisconsin, came from the Sir Robert Fossett Circus in England and was originally built for Lord George Sanger's famous show.*

Right: *The Chinese Acrobatic Theatre of Shanghai perform their tableau, 'Flying Flags'. Acrobats in China train for five years before appearing in front of the public.*

Left: *The Swiss National Circus Knie is one of the finest in the world. In 1978, to celebrate Knie's sixtieth year in circus and 175 years of the Knie dynasty, a big parade was held in each town on the tour. Brothers Rolf and Fredy Knie, the fifth generation of the family, and their sons Fredy, Rolf, Louis and Franco, run the circus today. They are justly famous throughout the world for their animals, which are superbly trained and presented with great charm and taste. The circus visits the same cities and towns each season and the programme is entirely changed for each tour.*

Right: *Norman Barrett is one of the most experienced ringmasters in circus today, having worked with the Bertram Mills Circus (until its closure as a touring circus in 1964 and at Olympia, London, until 1967), with Sweden's Circus Scott, at the Belle Vue Circus in Manchester and the Tower Circus in Blackpool. The red tail-coat was first introduced by Bertram Mills at Olympia and worn by the famous ringmaster George Lockhart in 1923. Prior to that, ringmasters often wore black or blue tail-coats.*

The circus audience also differs in various countries in the world. While it does appeal greatly to children, the circus is not a children's entertainment. The majority of the spectators at the evening performances of Circus Krone in Germany or the Moscow State Circus are adults whereas in Britain and America it is more a family audience. There's a saying in Britain that it can take four adults to take one child to the circus though, like the other popular entertainments, it can be said that the circus rarely receives the critical acclaim from the media that it deserves.

There have been two recent developments which have pinpointed the high standard of attainment of the world's top artistes. The International Circus Festival of Monte Carlo celebrated its sixth year in 1979. Established by Prince Rainier (a circus fan since the age of six), this week-long event brings together 45 of the world's top circus acts which appear in evening shows watched by, among others, a panel of distinguished judges. On the final evening, awards are made to the acts agreed to be particularly outstanding. These include a number of Silver Clown awards and one Gold Clown – the circus world's 'Oscars' – for contributions to all the circus arts of special merit. The Festival was established to heighten the public's awareness of the circus. It is shown on television in many countries of the world and, in 1979, a company of prize winners from the Festival toured North America under the auspices of the Ringling organization. In London in 1976, the Circus World Championships were staged for the first time. Here artistes competed in various categories and were awarded points by a panel of circus directors. Two acts in each category went forward into the final and the winner was declared Circus World Champion in his particular field. The aim of the Championships was to highlight the great athletic achievements of many circus acrobats – on the flying trapeze, high wire, springboard, etc. The organisers argued that the top circus artistes were as accomplished as the competitors in the Olympic Games. Never before had it been possible to watch

three or four of the greatest flying trapeze troupes in the world in order to judge which act was the finest. With the Circus World Championships, that dream became a possibility, although existing contracts to circuses at the time of the competition inevitably limit the numbers of artistes able to take part. The annual Championships involved a dozen circus skills and television shows of the events are seen all around the world.

Much of the success of any circus performance depends on the acts themselves but the surroundings, atmosphere and organization of the show also contribute enormously. The ringmaster is crucial to the smooth running of the live performance. He makes announcements and indulges in repartee with the clowns. He must stage manage the show, ensuring the ring boys set the props correctly and that each act works to time. He is also the link between the artistes and the management and may be called upon to sort out problems large and small. Norman Barrett of the Blackpool Tower Circus and the Belle Vue Christmas Circus in England is the epitome of a ringmaster, unflappable and always able to cover any temporary hitch in the running of the show with relaxed good humour. In America, on the gigantic Ringling circuses, the job, not surprisingly, is split, with a Performance Director (and his assistant) looking after the management of the show and a singing ringmaster making all the announcements. The lighting and the music are also vital to your enjoyment of the circus. After all, if there is a poor act, it's only in the ring for ten minutes, but if the band is mediocre, you have to endure it for the entire performance! The musical accompaniment for a circus is often as diverse as the acts themselves, ranging from dramatic classical pieces or traditional circus tunes like *The Entry of the Gladiators* to film or TV themes and disco music.

A good atmosphere, modern lighting and costuming and an efficient, fast moving presentation can be invaluable in your enjoyment of the various skills that have traditionally combined to produce the circus!

THE HORSES

The elements that make up the modern circus have their origins in ancient and medieval history. There were acrobats, jugglers and tumblers in ancient Egypt, Greece and Rome and the huge amphitheatres of Rome did feature some animal *training* as well as the horrendous carnage of man and animal. During the middle ages, the tradition of the travelling entertainer was continued but it was not until the late eighteenth century that the various types of display began to be combined and the circus as we know it today was established.

In the 1760s, various trick riders started giving exhibitions of their skill in gardens and fields in London. One of them, Sergeant-Major Philip Astley, a former dragoon, roped off a ring for his shows at Halfpenny Hatch, not far from the present site of Waterloo railway station. It is said that Astley decided to perform in a circular arena as centrifugal force helped him to keep his balance as he stood on the horse's back. The truth of this story is open to doubt just as lack of documentation leaves many aspects of the early history of the circus shrouded in mystery. It seems likely that this was one of the contributary factors leading to the development of the circus ring. Equally important, perhaps, was the fact that Astley trained his horses on a lunge as they circled him anti-clockwise and also, quite simply, that the crowds watching the performances would naturally try to form a circle so that everyone had a good view.

For sixpence a head, Londoners could enjoy trick-riding displays by Astley and his wife and their 'Little Military Learned Horse' entranced the crowds by striking the day of the month and the hour of the day with his hoof, laying down as if he were dead and then getting up and firing a pistol when ordered to fight for the Dragoons. Soon Astley added tumbling, acrobatic pyramid building and Fortunelly, the clown on the slack rope, to the programme.

Left: *Astley's Royal Amphitheatre of Arts in Westminster Bridge Road, London, in 1808. The performances at Astley's took place on stage and in the ring, there being 'Hippodramas', or melodramas on horseback, as well as the circus acts.*

Right: *The Mohawks, seen here at the 1977 Circus World Championships, are members of the Paulo family. Clara Paulo, her husband Ken MacManus, their daughter Evelyn and son-in-law John Darnell presented a rip-roaring display of bareback riding. They make their own elaborate costumes, with intricate beadwork and hand-tooled leatherwork.*

Right: *Six magnificent Lippizaner stallions on their hind legs at the Blackpool Tower Circus. Each horse will have been trained for this trick individually and gradually they will have been brought together to perform in unison. These Lippizaners come from Circus Knie in Switzerland which hires out some of its animals (and trainers) to other European circuses.*

Below: *Rolf Knie Junior is seen here in the early stages of the gruelling 'Courier of St. Petersburg' act. He is picking up the reins of the centre horse as it goes by. At another point in the act Rolf Knie allows two horses to pass beneath him, a feat which requires even greater strength and control over his cantering steeds.*

Below: *The Caroli family, from Italy, present one of the largest riding acts to be seen today, with ten riders. They specialize in the building of these human pyramids on horseback. They have a dozen horses in their stable. As well as their troupe act, members of the family can present pas-de-deux and solo ballerina routines on horseback. Brothers Enrico, Ernesto and Francesco Caroli, whose children are seen below, no longer ride but they are always on hand during the act to assist and Enrico stands in the centre of the ring to 'keep up' the horses – that is, to ensure they maintain an even gait.*

Astley's shows flourished and, in 1782, he and his company were invited to France to perform before the King and his Court. They delighted Marie Antoinette who arranged for them to return to give more shows. The circus in France subsequently became increasingly important and fashionable under the Franconi family. Another Englishman, Hughes, once in Astley's company but later one of his main rivals, took the circus to Russia where Catherine the Great had an arena built for him in the royal palace at St. Petersburg. And in 1793 the circus spread to America, where Bill Ricketts, one of Hughes's *protégés*, built a circus in Philadelphia.

Horses and trick riding were the core of the circus of those times and the horse remains a vital ingredient of today's programmes. The diameter of the ring has been standardised at 13 metres (42 feet) in most of the major circuses of the world

and this greatly helps horse and rider in the correct timing of their routines. Just a few feet can make a difference. When the Bratuchin troupe appeared at Billy Smart's Circus for a TV recording, they had come from a circus with a slightly smaller ring. The first practice resulted in confusion when the horses, bewildered by the change in surroundings, moved unevenly and once or twice even stopped altogether, proving dangerous for the riders who came off their mounts' backs. They quickly adjusted to the new ring, however, and the act then proceeded at its usual rip-roaring pace.

Various types of trick riding have evolved, influenced often by the riding style of the country. The most obvious example of this is the Cossack act so often seen at the State Circuses of Russia. Using a saddle on the horse, the rider throws himself off and on and even climbs around his mount with amazing speed,

raries was continued and developed into bareback riding. Whereas Russian and American trick riding evolved around the saddle, bareback riding involves no such prop – just a surcingle around the horse, with handles so that the rider can vault on to its back. Once there, he or she stands up and performs various jumps and somersaults. Further variety can be provided by more riders and horses and so the troupe bareback act developed, involving the building of precarious human pyramids of perhaps eight people on five horses. The Italian Cristiani family produced one of the finest of such acts. In the late 1930s, their routine included such gems as four of the men running and jumping to stand on a moving horse's back simultaneously. This trick performed by just one man is rarely seen today. During the 1920s and 1930s, the family circuses in Britain all included their own riding troupe. These included the Bakers and the Yeldings (who went on to work at the great Bertram Mills Circus), the Paulos, the Rosaires, the Kayes and the Fossetts (who were awarded many medals for their 'Champion Jockey Rider' performances) yet, sadly, today only members of the Paulo family (as the Mohawks) maintain this tradition.

Towards the end of the last century, many bareback riders began to dress as jockeys and even today they are often known as jockey riders. Incredible as it may seem now, in the 1880s it was quite usual for there to be more than one bareback riding number in a programme. There was often great rivalry amongst the various jockey riders. At the famous Circus Renz in Berlin, there were once no fewer than seven solo riders, according to the doyen of circus fans, Harry Nutkins, a man whose deep knowledge and interest has developed over his past 80 years of circus going. The last to appear, the Englishman Wilkes Lloyd, was not considered such a fine rider as the others but he gained the most applause because of the speed of his act. The jockey costume for a bareback riding act can now only be seen in France where the Gruss family present a superb display in their *Cirque à l'Ancienne* in the heart of Paris. Brothers Alexis and Patrick and their sister Martine commence the act at a lively pace which gradually quickens to a point where the two brothers are running up and jumping on and off their galloping steed both to an astride and to a standing position. Finally, a fast 'finish' horse is brought in. As it circles the ring Alexis stands on its back and unfurls an enormous flag.

Trick riding, of course, does not have to be so splendidly hectic. In the same programme, Alexis Gruss (who is the Principal of France's main circus school) and one of his pupils, Mary, appear in a graceful *pas de deux* on horseback, a routine requiring great strength and control as well as balance. The act of the Svennsons, from Sweden, commences in a similar vein with a classic display by a boy and girl rider on the backs of two beautifully matched grey horses. They are subsequently interrupted by two stooge 'members of the audience' whose comic antics in attempting to ride hides their very considerable ability. Real members of the audience are seen in two other forms of riding act. On the Riding Machine, you are invited to try to ride a circus horse being protected from injury by a safety harness. Secondly, there is the unrideable mule, whose wily stubbornness can be spectacularly exploited. When the act is as well presented as Helmbrecht and Karin Hoppe's act, the result can be hilarious.

The introduction of a rider from the audience was popularised by one of Astley's successors in London, Andrew Ducrow, who took over Astley's Amphitheatre in 1824. Ducrow was one of the finest performers of his time. He was immensely popular and his fame is reflected in the large number of prints published of him. He was also responsible for the development of the exacting riding number which is still seen today occasionally, 'The Courier of St. Petersburg'. In this, the rider stands astride two horses and others pass between them. The reins are snatched up as the horses pass underneath the rider so that eventually five or more are driven in front of the original pair. The act is so named since it was meant to represent the journey of a courier from England to

seeming to make an angle of 45 degrees between the horse and the ring at times. Such fast moving work is only possible when the animal can get a good grip on the ground and this is not feasible on the coconut matting used in many of the circus buildings of the world. So when the Iriston Caucasian Cossacks appeared with the Moscow State Circus at Belle Vue, Manchester, in 1971, the usual mat ring was removed and an earth one put in so that they could present their act effectively.

American trick riding, using a western saddle on the horse, probably had its heyday during the tours of Buffalo Bill's Wild West in the late nineteenth and early twentieth century. Colonel William Frederick Cody, alias 'Buffalo Bill', the most famous real-life Wild West hero, started his big arena shows in 1883. Although not presented in a circus ring, they have had a major influence on the circus, as indeed they have on film and television 'Westerns'. The attack on the Deadwood Stagecoach by Indians was the most celebrated of Cody's displays. When the show appeared in London in 1887, a special Royal Command show for Queen Victoria led to the coach having some very illustrious passengers, in the persons of the Kings of Saxony, Greece and Denmark and the Crown Prince of Austria. The Prince of Wales (later King Edward VII) rode shotgun and Cody himself drove! The touring of this show in Britain, France, Spain, Italy, Austria and Germany made it famous throughout Europe and soon the 'Congress of Rough Riders of the World' was added to its title. An 1896 programme, which incidentally features horses and riding in almost every display, lists the Congress as comprising, 'Indians, Cowboys, Mexicans, Cossacks, Gauchos, Arabs, Scouts, Guides, American Negroes and detachments of fully equipped Regular Soldiers of the Armies of America, England, France, Germany and Russia'. As well as cowboy style riding, various other western pastimes have been made into circus acts – rope spinning, whip cracking, knife throwing, etc. – and their appeal now is as strong as it was in the days of Buffalo Bill.

The English riding tradition of Astley and his contempo-

Left: *Katja Schumann, seen here with her chestnut Arab, Warrior, at the 1976 Circus World Championships, is a member of one of the most celebrated circus families. The dynasty was founded by Gotthold Schumann (1825–1908) and his great-grandchildren, Albert and Max, presented some superb liberty and High School horse acts at the great post-war London* *Christmas circuses – firstly at Tom Arnold's shows at Harringay arena and then at the Bertram Mills Circus at Olympia. During the summer months, their own Cirkus Schumann went on tour in Scandinavia and had a resident season at the circus building in Copenhagen. The original Schumann show closed in 1969, when Albert retired, but* *his younger brother Max started his own circus in 1977 with his wife Vivi, daughter Katja and son Philip. The Schumanns have married into other famous circus families. Albert is married to Paulina, daughter of the great Spanish clown Charlie Rivel, and his late sister, Cissie, was married to Britain's Johnny Kayes.* Above: *Tommy Roberts Junior (seen here with one of his ponies) is a member of one of the most versatile circus families. Tommy, his brother Bobby, sister-in-law Moira, cousins John, Tonya and Beverley are experts in over a dozen circus skills.*

Russia, the horses passing beneath him being the countries he goes through. Norman Barrett used to perform this rigorous act when with the Bertram Mills show in the early 1960s and more recently Rolf Knie of the Swiss Circus Knie has presented it. They gave it a Roman theme, dressing as legionary soldiers, as did Maurice Carré who followed in his father's footsteps by presenting this act in the 1950s. Now a director of the Boswell Wilkie Circus in South Africa, Maurice Carré is the great-grandson of Oscar Carré, who ran his own big touring show as well as the famous circus building in Amsterdam which bears his name. Although it is rarely used for circus presentations now, the Carré building is an attractive landmark in the city.

Horses used in riding acts need to be extremely steady in gait and to have a broad back. The riders currently seen in acts from the State Circuses of Hungary and Bulgaria also often use a pad on the back of the horse to help them to keep a firm footing. Although such displays (featured in three rings on the Blue Unit of the Ringling Circus) are inevitably slower than the jockey riding of, say, the Gruss family, they do include some spectacular pyramids and somersaults from horse to horse. The Hungarian Richter family, winners of the Silver Clown award at the Monte Carlo Circus Festival, are among the best acts of

this type. With three horses moving in file, two riders, on horses one and two, perform back somersaults, landing on horses two and three. They also feature an amazing head-to-head balance by two riders on a moving horse. One of them places a small circular 'doughnut' support on his head, the other does a headstand on this and the riders let go of each other's hands – a magnificent feat.

Riding of a different nature comes in High School, the circus world's version of dressage. All the basic movements are included, such as the *passage*, the *piaffe*, the march and the polka, and the circus band keeps in time with the horses' movements to accentuate the rhythm of the action. Sometimes the horses are said to be 'dancing' but this is not really the case. It is the bandmaster who keeps in time with the horse, rather than the other way round. During the nineteenth century, lady High School riders were amongst the most popular stars of the fashionable circuses in Paris and other European capitals.

The physical fitness required of the High School horse is considerable. James Fillis, one of the most celebrated trainers, published his *Breaking and Riding* in its original French edition at the request of Clemenceau in 1890. Fillis states that the strength and ability of his horses must be built up over a long

Right: *'An Equestrian Dream' was the title of this liberty horse act developed at Circus Knie and presented at the Blackpool Tower Circus by Franz Richard Althoff in 1976. This was a good example of how a traditional circus act can be made doubly effective by modern lighting, music – 'When will I see you again' – and production effects (the use of 'dry ice' gives the impression of clouds in the ring).*

Below: *The names of Mary Chipperfield's Arab stallions conjure up all the romance and mystery of the East – Baghdad, Sceptre, Sherif, Araby, Aurique, Imahn, Kismet and Emir. Mary herself was born in a caravan in Kentish Town, London, and she grew up on Chipperfield's Circus, surrounded by literally hundreds of exotic animals. Although horses will always occupy a special place in her affections, Mary has also trained tigers, lions, bears, leopards, elephants, chimps, zebras, llamas, and even giraffes, eland, yak, kangaroo and a pygmy hippopotamus. Mary and her sister Margaret have over 100 animals in their care which they present all over Europe and on their father's show, Jimmy Chipperfield's Circus World.*

period so that 'their muscles stand out and are as hard as steel and their general health is perfect'.

When the general use of the horse went into a decline with the arrival of the internal combustion engine, it is perhaps not surprising that High School riding was not appreciated so much by the public. But it is still seen in several major circuses of the world, particularly those with a strong equestrian tradition, such as Krone in Germany, Knie in Switzerland, Benneweis and Schumann in Denmark. In 1976, at the first Circus World Championships, staged in London, Katja Schumann, a member of the fifth generation of her family to work with horses in the circus, competed in the High School final against Britain's Mary Chipperfield. It was a close and exciting contest with Katja receiving 92 points out of 100 against Mary's 91. Katja's smooth flowing routine on the chestnut Arab, Warrior, was all the more charming for the music accompanying it – a selection of tunes made famous by Edith Piaf. She also rides side-saddle throughout. 'It's more difficult . . . but a lot prettier,' she says. In the 1978 Championships, Katja returned as a guest artiste and introduced a novel finale to her routine, jumping her horse over a dinner table at which revellers were enjoying a glass of champagne.

Today's High School routines are often presented as colourful spectacles linked to a country – Russia, Argentina, Spain – with suitable music and costumes. The Schumanns, the Knies and the Krones have been particularly effective here although the spectator tends to be dazzled by the presentation rather than being able to concentrate on the smooth interaction between horse and rider. For this, a single mount and rider are best, as with Fredy Knie Junior, who, in 1970, presented a routine with the Andalusian stallion, Parzi, during which the saddle and bridle were removed and the intricate routine repeated – a memorable sight.

While trick riding and High School acts are not so widespread as during the last century, the liberty horse troupe has on the whole maintained its place on today's circus programmes. Spectacular troupes of up to twenty-four horses in one ring have been seen but usually between four and twelve are shown. Larger groups are not only extremely costly to buy

Left: *Trick rider Michaela Kaiser was a member of her father's Golgojew Cossack Troupe, for many years featured on Germany's Circus Busch-Roland. In 1977, she left to form her own group, whose fast moving act has been presented in Norway, France and England. She is seen here competing in the Circus World Championships in London.*

and keep but much more difficult to present effectively. Liberty groups are assembled with great care, for each horse needs to be matched for temperament as well as colour with its neighbours. Mary Chipperfield spent nearly a year visiting Arab studs all over Britain when assembling her troupe of beautiful grey stallions.

Before the horses can be taught the complex liberty routines, each one must receive its basic training. On command, they must walk forward and stop on cue; walk backwards and stop; trot; gallop; and come out of file to the trainer in the centre of the ring. Although they will work freely in the finished act, during training the horses will often have riders to teach them the right position in each formation. In teaching a horse to walk on its hind legs, the trainer is exploiting a natural tendency for stallions to rear up when fighting. Nevertheless, each horse should be at least three years old before such training is started and the horse's confidence and physical ability need to be developed gradually.

Training a troupe of horses is a costly procedure and a lengthy one. Visiting the stables of one of the great circuses, like Circus Knie in Switzerland, however, shows the results of this patient and careful process in a beautiful collection of superbly fit horses and ponies, including Arabs, Friesians, Andalusians, apricot coloured Achal-Tekeyners, Danish tigerchecks, and grey Lippizaners, many of them over twenty years old.

The 'educated' horse or pony is especially beloved of the smaller circuses, where time-honoured routines have the pony 'telling fortunes', counting out the number of days in a week with its hoof, doing simple addition and subtraction sums and pointing out the biggest fool in the circus – invariably the trainer. Other artistes have made similar routines into suitable acts for larger circuses, among the most successful being Derrick Rosaire with his steed, Tony, and his niece, Joan, with Goldie, both horses being beautiful palominos. The continued presence of such numbers in today's shows is a fitting reminder of the 'Little Military Learned Horse' which was a feature of Astley's first shows.

Below: Fredy Knie Junior presents the liberty horses on his family's circus in Switzerland. This photograph emphasises the close involvement of the audience in what is happening in the ring. Unlike the theatre, there is no proscenium arch, no curtain, nothing to distance the performers from the spectators. Fredy Knie Junior is a gifted trainer and presenter of animals, especially horses. In this particular act, he shared the presentation of the horses with his attractive wife, Mary Jose (on the bandstand). Their daughter (a representative of the seventh generation of Knies) Géraldine-Katharina has inherited their love of horses. She appeared in a special children's show when only two and, in 1977, aged four, she appeared in the regular Knie performance with an act with a gigantic English shire horse, Major, and a tiny Argentinian dwarf pony, Chicito.

Right: Beautiful equestrienne Yasmine Smart is seen here with her Andalusian stallion in the 1978 Brighton Centre Circus. Yasmine, grand-daughter of the founder of Billy Smart's Circus, has her own liberty and High School horses and is well known throughout the world as the glamorous ringmistress on the Smart television shows. The late Billy Smart, who died in 1966, was a fun-fair operator who started his circus in 1946. A big man, with a big family of ten sons and daughters and countless grandchildren, his circus became Britain's biggest until rising costs forced it off the road in 1971. Yasmine, eldest daughter of David and Olga Smart, was tutored in horse training and presenting by John Gindl, whose career of over 60 years includes time with Hagenbeck, Bertram Mills and Billy Smart.

THE CLOWNS

The clown is one of the key people in the circus performance. He provides the essential comic relief from the tensions inevitably produced by such dangerous acts as the flying trapeze or walking the high wire. He is a link between the audience and the activity in the ring. In addition, his appearances can help to keep the show running smoothly by covering the setting up of props. The great American showman, Phineas T. Barnum, declared in the last century that clowns and elephants were the pegs on which the circus was hung and his proclamation remains as true today as it was then.

Clowns are often known as 'joeys' after the famous droll Joseph Grimaldi. He was, in fact, a pantomime clown and almost certainly never appeared in the circus, although his father was once ballet master at the Royal Circus in London, a rival to Astley's. The pantomime became fashionable in the London theatres early in the last century. The art had been adapted from the Italian Commedia dell'Arte (Comedy of Professional Actors) whose characters, Pantaloon, Columbine and Harlequin, were seen on the English fairground and subsequently in the theatre. The first pantomime was performed at Drury Lane in 1702 and, some fifty-six years later, Giuseppe Grimaldi was a dancer there in *The Miller*, a pantomime dance. His son, Joseph, became the most popular character in the English pantomime for some thirty years in the part of Clown, described by one contemporary writer as 'rascal and dupe, cunning and stupid all rolled into one'. In his costume reminiscent of the French pierrot and English jester, Joey was the perfect foil to the elegant Harlequin in love with Columbine. This mixture of cunning and stupidity is recognizable today in the relationship between the clowns and the ringmaster, or between the auguste (the clown with the bizarre make-up and baggy clothes) and the immaculate white face clown, whose costume is reminiscent of Harlequin's.

Left: *'Where is he?' shouts Jacko Fossett, while his midget partner, Little Paul, hides from him. Audience participation is an essential ingredient in successful clowning, yet it takes an expert like Jacko Fossett to achieve it in an arena as big as this one at the National Exhibition Centre in Birmingham. Jacko, previously a trapeze artiste, tumbler and rider, became known as 'Kangaroo Jack' when he specialized in acting as sparring partner for a boxing kangaroo. His former partner, Little Billy Merchant, retired in 1978 but he stayed with Jacko for six months in order to advise his replacement, teenager Paul.*

Above: *American Phil Enos has one of the most explosive of all comedy cars. Doors fall off, loud bangs come from under the bonnet and the radiator has a penchant for alcohol!*

Right: *Toulouse Lautrec was a great lover of the Parisian circuses during the late nineteenth century. He produced a series of 39 drawings on the circus (including this one, entitled 'Performing Horse and Monkey') in 1899, while recovering in a rest home in Neuilly from a serious breakdown. The famous clowns Footit and Chocolat were friends of Toulouse Lautrec and feature in many of his works. Footit became a clown after he lost his horse while playing poker at the Paris Hippodrome where he was engaged as a rider. Toulouse Lautrec's passion for the circus was shared by other great painters, among them Degas, Picasso, Rouault and Chagall. The circus was a highly fashionable entertainment during this period. Members of the aristocracy were often seen there and the Jockey Club had a box at the Nouveau Cirque. The impresario C. B. Cochran recalled being taken to clown Footit's 'loge' where he met Debussy and Toulouse Lautrec.*

John Ducrow, brother to the illustrious rider Andrew, was quick to adapt Grimaldi's whimsicalities to Astley's ring, using his make-up and costume. Other clowns also produced variations on Joey's transport – he was pulled across the stage in a small cart by a team of dogs. One was pulled in a tub by geese or in a cart by cats. Much later, the transport theme was continued with cars becoming a favourite prop for clowns. Exploding engines and jets of water from the radiator struck a chord with many members of the audience who had suffered from similar, if not so spectacular, recalcitrance from their automobiles. Even the car has now been updated in space ship routines, such as the one performed by Jacko Fossett and Little Billy.

As the circus was primarily an equestrian entertainment in its early days, the clown was often seen in the role of comedy rider, involved in lots of backchat with the ringmaster. His nonsense was useful as a break from the more serious, strenuous feats of horsemanship. When the lady ballerina on horseback appeared, the clown was her suitor and this routine became as much a part of the circus as the sawdust in the ring. Much of the clown's routine involved talking and this went down well in the intimate purpose-built circus buildings of the time. Some clowns even went so far as to recite passages from Shakespeare and poetry with moral and political undertones. One of these, W. F. Wallett, gave himself the title of the 'Queen's Jester' after taking four lion cubs to show to Queen Victoria at Windsor Castle. In America, Dan Rice was known as 'Lincoln's Jester'. He is said to have befriended the President and cultivated a beard in order to look like him. At the height of his career, Rice was the subject of a draft movement to be democratic nominee for President. At his lowest, he lectured on the dangers of alcohol in between acts in his own circus, with a bottle of spirits hidden under his lectern. The traditional talking clown has disappeared now, except occasionally in small 'tenting' (under canvas) circuses. The major shows of today require bigger clown routines altogether and talking is almost always kept at a minimum.

The clown who receives all the custard pies and the water, the one with the grotesque make up, baggy clothes and large boots, is known as an 'Auguste' (a colloquial German name

inferring bumbling idiocy). The inventor of this style of clowning is said to have been Tom Belling, a young American rider who was appearing at Circus Renz in Berlin in 1869. The Renz show was well known for the perfection of its equestrian numbers. Failing to do a simple trick, Belling was punished by the strict proprietor, Ernest Renz, by being banned from the ring for a month. One night during a performance, for sheer devilment, Belling donned a riding jacket inside out and put a wig on back to front, with the hair tied to make it stand on end. Looking in the mirror, he decided the effect was so funny that he would show himself to his fellow artistes. He had no sooner left the dressing room than he ran into the obdurate Renz, who, out of character, saw the humour of the situation and pushed the startled Belling into the ring. He promptly fell on his face. The cries of 'Auguste' and the laughter which followed set the seal on a new career for Belling and a new type of clown was born.

Clowning gained particular popularity in the circus buildings in Paris at the end of the last century. The diminutive James Guyon was a popular auguste at the Paris Hippodrome, a feat indeed when one considers that the main attractions of this spacious building were chariot racing and wild animal presentations. In the more intimate Nouveau Cirque, Footit, the white face clown, and Chocolat, the auguste, were a great success. Footit was the son of an English circus proprietor. His role was to be pigheaded and ill-natured to Chocolat, a lazy, good-for-nothing, played by a Cuban acrobat. The pair were the subject of many of Toulouse Lautrec's sketches and set the pattern for clown duos in France. They made use of the sinking ring at the Nouveau Cirque which was flooded for sketches such as *The Wedding Party*, in which members of a village wedding gathering were thrown bodily into the water. In England's Blackpool Tower Circus, the flooded ring has been used to good effect by Charlie Cairoli and Company. Charlie, who was born in Milan, first appeared at the Tower in 1939. He is one of the most inventive clowns in the business today. With his father, he received the best possible training at the Cirque Medrano in Paris where, between 1927 and 1937, they devised over 700 routines, since the programme was changed so regularly. Like many European clowns, Charlie is a talented musician. He preforms two acts, or entrées as they are known, in each Blackpool programme, one musical and one slapstick. He is joined in both by his son, Charlie Junior, the white face clown, and Jimmy Buchanan, who has been at the receiving end of more buckets of water than he would care to remember. Charlie Cairoli's wife is a member of another famous French clowning family – the Frattellini.

The Trio Frattellini were the most celebrated group of clowns in the history of the circus. These three sons of Gustav Frattellini raised the whole standard of the Parisian circuses from their first appearance at the Cirque Medrano in 1918. Their crowning hour must have been when they appeared at the Comédie Francaise, one of the most honoured institutions in France. Good timing, beautiful costuming and brilliant musicianship were their hallmark – a tradition carried on today by such troupes as the Francescos, the Morenos, the Rastelli (whose act has featured a Chocolate character) and the Barios.

Albert Frattellini's grotesque make-up, with its large exaggerated mouth and raised eyebrows, was an inspiration to many clowns, including Lou Jacobs, the American clown pictured on a USA postage stamp. This seventy-seven-year-old star of the Ringling Circus Red Unit is an ex-contortionist. He always used to raise a laugh when he extracted his large body (made to look even bigger by his heavy coat and outsize boots) from inside his miniature car. Many other clowns have copied this make-up but no one could copy his car routine. With the large arenas of the three ring circuses, clowning in America developed a character all of its own, requiring large numbers of clowns, with more colourful clothes and more exaggerated make up than their European counterparts. The comic armies which ran in and out between the acts kept on getting in the way of the other artistes as they congregated around the performers' entrance, so they were given their own dressing room tent, adjoining the big top, which became known as 'Clown Alley'. The traditional clown entrée of the Ringling Circus, 'Fireman, save my child!', is still a part of this show, with lots of clowns and finally a mother and baby appearing from a burning house to be rescued by a team of clown firemen who arrive on a variety of fire engines. The Americans also developed a specialized type of clowning in which clowns played to a small section of the audience from the hippodrome track. The best known of these – Otto Griebling and Emmett Kelly, both now dead – were tramp clowns. The key to Kelly's dead-pan character was his pathos. He amused his audience by lighting a fire to warm his hands, munching a cabbage, attempting to crack a peanut with a 40-lb sledgehammer and sweeping up the spotlight with a battered broom. Kelly's hobo character was invented by him for a newspaper cartoon and he has been succeeded by his son. Michael Coco, son of the famous Russian-born clown Coco, beloved of patrons of the Bertram Mills Circus in Britain, is another current American clown favourite. His late father was awarded the OBE for his services to road safety. He spent many hours visiting schools and talking to children on the subject. Clowns are often used by the producers of a circus to divert the audience's attention while the props are being changed for the next act. Such clowns are known as run-in clowns. The finest of them often parody the acts they follow. This is the formula successfully employed by Oleg Popov, Mi and Anatol Martchevsky of the State Circuses of Russia while the East

Right: *Clowns Sonny Fossett and Matto present one of the favourite entrées – 'The Haunted House'. The clowns are appointed caretakers to an old house by the ringmaster, who, ominously, informs them that it is haunted. Well routined, the theme can prove to be highly* *successful, with ghosts, giant spiders and moving skeletons adding to the fun, as in this version, seen on Gerry Cottle's Circus in England. Matto, incidentally, is a young newcomer to circus, Matthew Ware.*

German clowns Jules and Bubi have proved a hit in European shows with inventive gags between the acts. They also have a longer entrée where they attempt to paint the roof of the circus and in which Jules is only saved from falling to the ring by his long elastic braces held by his partner.

The majority of circus clowns are not well known to the general public and consequently they have to work hard initially to establish a rapport with the audience. A few clowns, such as the Barios in France, or the diminutive Tickey (named after South Africa's smallest coin) or Charlie Cairoli in England, are sufficiently famous in their own countries to be warmly welcomed when they appear. The Swiss Circus Knie has, in recent years, often booked the comedy element of its programme from other sections of showbusiness – Emil, the

well-known television comedian, and Dimitri, the famous mime artiste who trained under Marcel Marceau. Emil proved to be the hit of the 1977 show, a quite outstanding achievement when you consider that it included the finest equestrian, wild animal and acrobatic acts. In an audience participation spot, he took on the role of ringmaster and had the children riding on adults' backs as if they were jockey riders. He even had children rolling over in the sawdust, emulating Louis Knie's rollover tigers. Dimitri performs two lengthy solo acts when he works in the theatre. On Circus Knie in 1973, he worked in between the acts, juggling, presenting an amazing pot-bellied pig, a routine with a brilliant yellow car, and even one with a black-and-white cow, complete with Swiss cow bells, which he eventually rode round the ring bareback.

Left: *Swiss duo the Chickys are one of the most famous European clown acts today. Chicky, the auguste, began his career in a small family circus as an aerial acrobat. At the age of 17, he had his own comic routine. In 1957, Chicky's cousin, Bruno, became a white face clown and their partnership has been highly successful.*

Right: *Professor Grimble (Tommy Fossett) is a lively clown character who is 'sacked' from the circus by his attractive wife, Vera. A former trapeze artiste, Tommy is also an accomplished juggler, unicyclist and musician.*

Below: *The Trio Francescos – Enrico, Ernesto and white face clown Francesco – are three of Europe's best musical clowns. Their children are the Carolis riders – see page 16.*

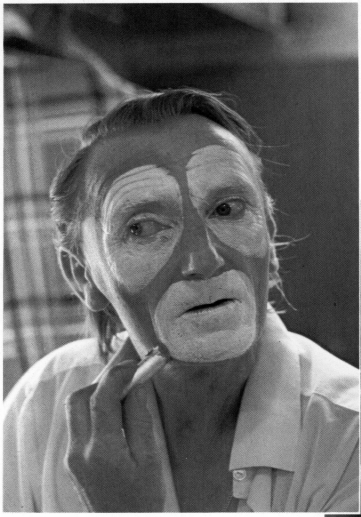

Sonny Fossett, seen here at three stages of applying his make-up, is principal clown on Gerry Cottle's Circus. The Fossett family is enormous and can rightly be described as the backbone of the British circus. Four of the circuses in England are run by members of the Fossett dynasty, including the Robert Brothers Circus and Sir Robert Fossett's Circus (one of the oldest established in the world, with headquarters in Northampton). There's a branch of the family running Fossett's Circus in Ireland. In addition, Gerry Cottle's wife, Betty, is a Fossett and, during 1979, there were Fossetts in circuses in America, South Africa and Hungary.

Today's circus programmes are faster moving than those of the past and the lengthy entrées once worked by the Frattellinis and their contemporaries so brilliantly would probably today not be so successful. Grock, the Swiss clown generally recognized as the most celebrated of them all, performed a routine lasting an hour in his own circus. The pathos wrung out of a simple situation by Grock – such as moving the grand piano towards the stool rather than the reverse – and the Russian clown Karandash and his efforts to re-build the five parts of a female statue are examples of moments of clowning to be savoured, but sadly they are rarely seen today.

Clowns also appear in other acts and the combination of clowning on the wire has been very successful. In the guise of the simple-hearted fellow doing his best, Popov balances on the slack wire and, like his childhood idol, Charlie Chaplin, works with the cane and bowler hat. Pio Nock, a member of the Swiss wire-walking dynasty, performs crazy antics on the high wire over an open cage of lions – an act which has the same sort of appeal as Buster Keaton's antics on the ledge of a skyscraper in the days of silent movies. Incidentally, Keaton clowned at the Cirque Medrano in Paris after he had retired from films, while

Chaplin appeared in his youth with Marceline at the London Hippodrome. The general demise of riding acts means that clowns on horseback are rarely seen today. The great Pimpo, of Sanger's Circus, used to appear in almost every act, including the flying trapeze, and was a great comedy rider, as was 'Poodles' Hannaford. He is remembered in circus circles for his step off the back of a galloping horse, in which he appears to be suspended in mid-air, as well as for his distinctive dress of ankle-length fur coat and a bowler hat.

Anxieties about the future of clowning in the circus have led to the establishment of training courses for would-be clowns. There are two circus schools teaching clowning in Paris. Ringlings run a clowns' college for an annual seven-week course. Over 40,000 people have applied since its commencement in 1968 and over 600 students have graduated. Men and women from all walks of life have gone through the course which includes in its curriculum make-up, costume, slapstick, mime, juggling and unicycling, taught by Ron Severini and his wife, Sandy, Deans of Clown College. One of the successful applicants, Peggy Lenore Williams, was a college graduate who majored in pathology and has achieved remarkable results

Left: *The ringmaster is often involved in clown entrées. He is the figure of authority in contrast to the wily absurdities of the clowns themselves. Here clown Gary is seen with ringmaster Chris Barltrop on Jimmy Chipperfield's Circus World. Gary is an accomplished juggler and musician, playing the guitar, clarinet, saxophone and bagpipes. His father, Noe-Noe, is a master of tomfoolery and slapstick who began his career as a young lad at the Tower Circus in his home town of Blackpool. Starting as an elephant groom, he tried his hand at various acts before finding his niche in comedy. Noe-Noe has proved that it is possible for an outsider to carve himself a career in the circus. His hilarious act has been seen all over Europe – from Norway to Poland.*

teaching mentally retarded and deaf children by means of pantomime. Another budding lady clown just wanted a change from pounding a typewriter.

'Clowns of America', formed in the same year as Ringlings started its college, is an organization 'dedicated to the perpetuation of the art of clowning' and one of its members was the famous comedian Red Skelton. In 1971, they helped to have a law passed which resulted in President Nixon signing a proclamation naming 1–7 August as National Clown Week. In England, Clowns International gathers together its members at the Holy Trinity Church, Dalston, London, every year to remember the original 'joey', Joseph Grimaldi.

Clowns and clowning will never die but the suggestion is often made that clowns are exclusively for children. Perhaps the best answer to this proposition is made by Dick Hurran, producer of the Blackpool Tower Circus, which has starred Charlie Cairoli for the past forty years: 'Just look at the sheer joy and excitement on the faces of the children as they shout, scream, jump and totally lose themselves in the magic world of fantasy and make-believe that Charlie creates for them. Then – and only then – look at the faces of the grown-ups ... I'll guarantee that every one of them is having as much fun as their offspring. Their enjoyment is not just from watching the antics of Charlie and his gang but in seeing and sharing that abundance of happiness that is all around them.'

Above: *Many of the finest clowns are also excellent musicians and Charlie Cairoli and his son, Charlie Junior, are no exceptions. Using their trumpets, trombones, clarinets and saxophones, they can produce a variety of curious, effective – and rude – sounds as well as playing a vast repertoire of tunes 'straight'. They play xylophones and hand bells and even invent their own unusual instruments, such as a kitchen sink and a length of rubber tubing, which they play a tune on. As well as being a most able musician, Charlie Cairoli is highly inventive and it is this quality – both in the devising of new entrées and in his ability to take advantage of any ad lib situation that presents itself – that has made him and his company (including Jimmy Buchanan, a wonderful stooge) so outstandingly successful.*

TOGARE AND

TO BE SEEN ONLY AT THE
GREAT CARMO CIRCUS

IS LIONS

MENAGERIE

THE BIG CAGE

Among the most popular animals which appear in the circus are the beautiful and potentially dangerous lions, tigers, leopards and bears which are presented in the dramatically named big cage, built up in the ring. Such performances have their origins in the ancient world with the appearance of the first collections of wild animals in captivity. Probably the most extraordinary group of animals ever assembled was paraded in the middle of the first millenium BC in Egypt by Ptolemy II on the occasion of the feast of Dionysus. It included 96 elephants, a giraffe, a rhinoceros, 24 lions and 14 leopards. Edward Campbell, a London journalist with a great knowledge of wild animals, has commented, 'It is inconceivable that such an operation could be mounted without people truly knowledgeable about animal behaviour being present and in charge.' There were wild animal trainers in ancient Rome too and a feat commonly described is that of harnessing a pair of lions to pull a chariot. During medieval times, there were a few royal menageries. In England, Henry I developed a small collection at Woodstock, a village near Oxford, which Henry III transferred to the Tower of London in the middle of the 13th century, where it remained for 600 years. Showmen first began to travel with wild beast shows to fairs in the eighteenth century – Pidcock's was one of them – but these were purely zoological exhibitions. It was probably not until around 1820 that a man entered the lions' cage of a European menagerie and re-discovered what the trainers of the ancient world so obviously understood – that a wild animal becomes tamer given gentle treatment and, furthermore, that it can be trained to do simple tricks on command. Whether the first man to do this was the Frenchman, Henri Martin, or the Englishman, 'Manchester Jack', of Wombwell's Menagerie, is open to question. The latter was in future years described as entering the cage of the fine old lion Nero, sitting on the animal's back and then opening his mouth.

Left: *Lion trainer Togare was a glamorous personality of the 1920s and 1930s. Dubbed 'The Valentino of the Ring', he appeared in the circus run by illusionist, the Great Carmo, in association with Bertram Mills in 1929. Carmo went it alone the following winter, losing one big top through snow and another in* *a fire on 20 March 1930 in Birmingham. There was no loss of life but the lions were burned when canvas fell on to their cages. Togare heroically calmed them and went in amongst them to treat their burns. In later years, his dramatic tiger act was a feature of the Bertram Mills Circus.*

Atkins, another menagerie owner of the time, advertised a lion and a tigress who had produced hybrid cubs at the Bartholomew Fair of 1825. Their keeper obviously had a good relationship with them as later descriptions of his performance testify. Both animals jumped through a hoop held by him. He would thrust his face down into the lion's throat and, finally, the lion would lie down, the man would lie on top of him and the tigress would then jump on him and lie with her paws upon his shoulders and her face sideways upon his. In 1832, the family was at Astley's and the trainer introduced the playful cubs to the audience. It is interesting that, 150 years later, the Chipperfield family, whose roots are in the menagerie business, bring lion and tiger cubs into the audience for souvenir photographs taken with a Polaroid camera.

On the other side of the world in America, a year after Atkins's showing at Astley's, Isaac van Amburgh, a Dutch American whose grandfather was a Red Indian, was making his début at the Richmond Hill Theatre in New York with a lion, tiger, panther and leopard. He later came to England and created a sensation. He gave his performance a quasi-religious aura by appearing in a gladiator costume and showing a lion and a lamb together. Queen Victoria was so intrigued that she saw van Amburgh's performance six times. His fame was also helped by the exhibition of Landseer's painting of him and his animals at the Royal Academy. Van Amburgh's tour of England and Scotland in the 1840s was the first undertaken by a circus with wild animals in a tent. The *Nairnshire Telegraph* described the performance as follows: 'After a demonstration

of the giraffe, van Amburgh, dressed as Rollo, with a whip in hand, dashed through the back door into one of the cages, of which a lioness, a tiger, and three beautiful leopards were the occupants. He was saluted by a savage growl from the tiger, who stood erect on his hind legs against the bars of the cage, while the lion maintained a dignified appearance and the leopards continued to gambol around the den. Van Amburgh appeared to be in his element among those dread rulers of their native forests, whom he sometimes hugged, teased, cuffed and pushed about. Leaving the den, he entered another with whose rough inmates he used the same familiarity and actually put his face into a lion's mouth; during all of which the spectators could scarce repress a shudder of horror.' In Europe, Henri Martin also showed a variety of wild animals and, like van

Amburgh, had melodramas written for him. On the stage of the Porte Saint Martin theatre in Paris, he played a part which required him to fight tigers, lions and hyenas with his bare hands, working behind a huge wire mesh screen which covered the front of the stage.

This type of performance – with the trainer usually going into the animals' living dens – was seen in travelling menageries during the last century and in England and France right up until the 1930s. When Carl Hagenbeck introduced the big circular cage to show wild animals in 1888, he was able to change the whole emphasis away from the bravery of the trainer to the beauty and agility of the animals. This principle is echoed today by Dick Chipperfield Junior who states, 'We are not showing how brave we are in the ring. We are just

Left: *Mary Chipperfield's leopard, Ikon, makes a spectacular picture in this jump featured in the 1979 Blackpool Tower Circus. The leopard was included in a group containing two lions, two tigers and a black bear. Such a group provides a fascinating opportunity to contrast these four different species.*

Above: *Dick Chipperfield Junior allows three black panthers and a leopard to lie on top of him. (The leopard and panther are in fact the same species, the variation being purely one of colour). Two of these animals are males and two females and this mixing of sexes compounds the danger. If a female is in season, this can give rise to squabbles between the cats as seen here. Chipperfield's rapport with them was such that one panther allowed him into her den to inspect her newly-born cubs.*

displaying the intelligence of the animals we train.' Carl Hagenbeck was born in 1844, the son of a Hamburg fishmonger whose sideline was dealing in wild animals. Carl became the largest animal dealer in the world and established his own zoo at Stellingen, showing animals in as near natural surroundings as possible, with moats and ditches instead of bars. His zoo park was an inspiration to many other zoo directors and its natural progression has been the drive-through safari parks first introduced by Jimmy Chipperfield at Longleat in England in 1966.

In Carl Hagenbeck's book *Beasts and Men*, published in 1919, he tells of his disgust with some of the displays with wild animals which he had seen during the last century where the trainer's fear and ignorance had led him to use brute force to try to control his lions and tigers. Following in the footsteps of Manchester Jack and Henri Martin, he instituted a more rational and humane method of training which was widely adopted. He reasoned that the wild animal's mind was basically the same as a human being's. Treated cruelly, the animal would retaliate with vicious hatred. Treated fairly, using Hagenbeck's 'gentling' method, it would respond with trust. He also emphasized that it was important to start the process when the animals were still young and to remove unsuitable characters from the group. His first trainer, Deyerling, successfully trained four lions using this method, having picked his quartet from a total of twenty-one.

The popular concept of the lion 'tamer', as seen in children's books and cartoons, is of a large moustached man dressed in an outfit similar to that of an army officer of the Kaiser brigade. This image was matched by Herr Seeth, a lion trainer of the

Above: *This polar bear on Chipperfield's Circus is demonstrating its natural ability to balance on a moving object. Other species of bear, amongst them brown Russian, Canadian black and Himayalan black bears (which have a white V mark on their chests), are also seen in the big cage or outside it on leads (see chapter eight). Dick Chipperfield Junior, who presents the bears on his family circus, is one of the best and most prolific of wild animal trainers, also working with lions, tigers, leopards and black panthers.*

Right: *This imposing 'family group' was photographed at the turn of the century in New York. Captain Jack Bonavita is seen with no less than thirteen magnificent lions, part of a group of twenty-seven he trained for Frank C. Bostock's Jungle Arena. On one occasion, some of the lions started fighting in the runway into the arena. Bonavita attempted to stop them but was himself injured and lost a hand and had to spend sixteen weeks in hospital for his pains.*

Hagenbeck school at the turn of the century. He appeared at the opening of the London Hippodrome on 15 January 1900, with his twenty-one lions. These handsome black-maned animals were presented to him by the Emperor Menelik of Abyssinia. The following day, *The Times* reported he was 'undoubtedly the sensation of the evening'.

Many wild animal trainers have in fact been smaller in stature than average and, unlike many circus performers, they are not often born into the business. A sensation of the 1920s and 1930s was the diminutive Captain Schneider and his lions. The rank of captain was bestowed on him by the King of the Belgians. Seventy lions were advertised when he appeared at

Above: *Both tigers and lions
have been taught to ride on
horseback, as in this act with a
tiger which was presented by
Mary-Jose and Fredy Knie
Junior on Circus Knie in 1978.
The tiger stands on a heavy pad
on the horse's back and the horse
wears protective covering on its
neck and flanks. It took two
years of patient training to
perfect the routine.*

Right: *Veteran lion trainer
Captain Sydney Howes retired
from the big cage in August
1979, just a few weeks after this
photograph was taken, at the age
of 69. This remarkable circus
man has spent his entire working
life among animals, with the
exception of army service during
the war. He left school at the age
of twelve to join G.B.
Chapman's animal dealing*

*business based in Tottenham
Court Road, London. When
Chapman branched into a
travelling menagerie and into
circuses, the young Sydney
Howes became apprenticed to
animal trainer, Jan Doksansky,
later presenting polar bears, then
lions, tigers and elephants. After
the war, Sydney Howes joined
Robert Brothers' Circus and
trained and presented groups of*

*their lions all over Europe. In
1973, he moved to the Cottle &
Austen Circus and he has
remained with the same group,
now owned by Gerry Cottle's
Circus, ever since. His daughter,
Barbara, and he present a chimp
act. Tragically his son, Gordon,
was killed by lions in 1978 in
Dublin – he inadvertently backed
into a lion, which, feeling
threatened, attacked him.*

the Bertram Mills Circus at Olympia, London, in 1925–6. The full collection could be seen in their dens and Schneider went in their midst, inspecting them for minor wounds and applying white ointment after feeding time. In the actual circus, the adult animals were sent into the big cage 'as easily as driving a flock of sheep', to quote a report in the showbusiness newspaper, *The World's Fair*, at the time. Three large baskets, which contained about ten lion cubs, were also displayed. As the finale of the performance, Schneider amazingly fed his lions with meat. He impressed the Society for the Prevention of Cruelty to Animals by showing his lions without a stick or whip. Olympia was also the scene of Alex Kerr being handed the conductor's baton from the orchestra to work his wild animal act some thirty years later, an event viewed with pleasure by Her Majesty the Queen.

Lion training in the early years of this century was by no means an exclusively male preserve. Tilly Bebe was a beautiful young girl whose affection for her lions was returned by the animals themselves. It was said they behaved like lovers, vying with each other for a caress from their mistress. Tilly Bebe was courted by plenty of male suitors but her overwhelming passion for the lions made her turn them all down. Sad to relate, she died in loneliness and poverty, still believing in her old age that she would once again enter the big cage.

Lions are the species of big cat most often seen in the circus. Their presentation takes two contrasting forms – *en ferocité* and *en pelotage*. The first is designed to show off the ferocious power of the lion in attack. The trainer needs to be a good actor to make it convincing, encouraging his animals to make mock charges at him, growling and roaring. *En pelotage* is a quieter,

more stylized form of showing the grace and beauty of movement of the big cats, requiring the trainer to work more closely with the animals, and said to be more dangerous. The late Clyde Beatty, celebrated for his appearances with Ringlings and later with his own show, fought off his animals with the help of a kitchen chair and the snarling of his beasts was accompanied by his firing of blank cartridges from a revolver. Beatty, who died in 1965, was a household name in his heyday but his act would appear melodramatic and old fashioned now. In contrast to the fighting style, Gerd Siemoneit presents a group of male lions on his own Circus Barum in Germany with such charm, almost boyish enthusiasm, that the audience is lulled into forgetting the danger that undoubtedly exists.

Wild animal trainers compare the nature of a lion with that of a dog whereas that of the tiger is likened to the domestic cat. Lions have been known to attack a trainer *en masse* but tigers are lone animals and would attack singly. Both tigers and lions breed well in captivity. Chipperfield's Circus in England has often successfully raised over thirty cubs a year, for example, and thirteen out of fifteen tigers in Charly Baumann's group of the Ringling show were bred by him. Alex Kerr of the Bertram Mills Circus gave an insight into the training of tigers in his book, *No Bars Between*, published in 1957. Kerr studied each tiger as a youngster to find out if it had a natural aptitude for any particular type of work. He observed, for example, that tall animals found it more difficult to achieve balancing feats than small ones. When he began training, with the tigers aged around 18 months when they are no longer cubs, he saw himself as the leader, or boss animal, of the group – in effect, a tiger among tigers. They regarded his whip or stick (used to

manoeuvre the animals in a particular direction) as an extension of his own limbs and not as a separate object.

The beauty of the tiger was effectively displayed by Richard Sawade, Hagenbeck's principal trainer from the 1880s to 1919. Dressed as an Indian rajah, he worked his animals *en pelotage*, showing their graceful forms in magnificent leaps from pedestal to pedestal, and he posed pyramid groupings which became an example to every other trainer. Amongst his pupils was Rudolph Matthies whose group of eight Bengal tigers was the first big cage presentation on the Ringling Brothers and Barnum & Bailey combined shows in 1919.

Close relationships of friendship and trust between some big cats and their trainers result in effective accomplishments in the circus. American Mabel Stark changed her occupation from nursing to wrestling with tigers. She was still pursuing her career, dressed in her famous outfit, a white leather suit, when she was well into her seventies. Tigers have no fear of water as proved by Margarita Nazarova of the Moscow State Circus when she swam with a tiger in a pool in the circus ring. Mary Chipperfield was more afraid of heights than her favourite tiger, Tigger, when she developed a trick whereby they were hoisted high above the circus ring on a small platform. The Naumanns, father and son, have a famous act in which a tiger jumps 20 feet into a pool of water.

The smaller cats – leopards, black panthers and pumas – are not so frequently seen as lions and tigers. They seem less impressive because of their size but in reality they are far harder to train, being extremely alert and quick to attack if flustered. Dick Chipperfield Junior produced a masterpiece of an act with three leopards and five black panthers which he trained while his family's circus was on tour in South Africa. It came to England for the first time in 1967 and was subsequently seen at the Ringling Circus in the USA, at the Cirque d'Hiver in Paris, the Krone-bau in Munich, Circus Knie in Switzerland, Circus Busch-Roland in Germany and at the Blackpool Tower Circus in England. Spending hour after hour with his young leopards in training, Chipperfield developed a routine remarkable for the closeness between man and animal. A man falling to the ground is likely to induce the natural reaction in a wild animal to attack, but Dick Chipperfield successfully trained four of his charges to lie on top of him as he lay on the floor of the ring. One of his black panthers jumped from one pedestal to another, using the trainer's arched back as a 'stepping stone' in between. Such a jump is remarkable as the panther would naturally regard a man in this position as prey but, because of his close relationship with Chipperfield, he did not attack. Dick Chipperfield's success with his leopards and black panthers was not without accidents, when one of the cats would lose its temper and lash out with its razor-sharp claws or teeth. Chipperfield has described the feeling of being attacked as being similar to having a hyperdermic needle violently jabbed into your skin and twisted. More recently, a large group of leopards, black panthers and pumas – nineteen in all – has been trained by Ringling circus superstar, Gunther Gebel-Williams, whose routine also features very close work with his animals, such as a lie-down and jump similar to those described above. It also includes some truly amazing jumps by leopards leaping enormous distances across the cage.

Bears are sometimes seen in the big cage and, of the various species, the polar bear is the most eye-catching. Bears have a good sense of balance and the circus feat of rolling a globe or a barrel can be seen as an extension of the polar bear keeping himself afloat on fast-moving ice floes in the wild. Wilhelm Hagenbeck's troupe of bears, most of them polars, allegedly numbered seventy at the turn of the century. They were announced, in the *World's Fair*, as opening at the London

Right: *Swiss trainer René Strickler needs to have complete confidence in the tiger and lioness to be able to perform this trick. Strickler's mixed group, comprising three tigers, three lionesses, two black Baribal bears, two pumas, two black panthers and two St. Bernard dogs, is one of the finest currently in Europe and it's notable for the playful relationship between trainer and animals. Like many trainers, Strickler was not born into the circus. Another outsider was John Benham, a young solicitor who gave up the legal profession to train and present the lions on Austen Brothers' Circus in England. An overwhelming interest in the circus and a love of wild animals in particular led John Benham into this potentially dangerous profession, but what were his feelings when he went into the cage for the first time? He writes, 'Before going in, I obviously felt very nervous, as I was being introduced to the lions by their original trainer, Brian Austen. Once inside, it was a great relief to discover that I did not feel any fear at such close proximity. On the contrary, it was great to see the lions with no bars in the way. The cage did not seem to shrink once I was inside, nor did the lions appear to double in size, as I had read.' After much practising, John Benham was ready to present the lions at a public performance, and he has subsequently developed his own style of showmanship in the big cage. Yet what is the great appeal for John Benham of lion training? He claims, 'The actual performance to me is only an excuse, a way of being able to work so closely with such fantastic animals, in their training and looking after them. I enjoy training sessions most of all, when the lions are at their most attentive, awake and alert because they are learning something new. I've never been afraid of them, although one has to have great respect, for they are still wild animals and could injure me, possibly without realising.'*

Left: *This young tiger is being trained by Carl Fischer on the Robert Brothers Circus to walk along two wires covered with thick rope. It was enticed up to the high end pedestal using small pieces of meat and then gradually was persuaded along the wire. Although it has done this trick several times in practice, it will still be many months before the trainer considers the tiger confident enough to perform it in public.*

Hippodrome on Boxing Day 1909. They were to close their performance by sliding down a chute into the Hippodrome water tank. A 1911 poster for the Blackpool Tower Circus lists Willy Hagenbeck's forty polar bears as appearing in the water at the circus, which must have been a staggering sight, especially when you remember that the diameter of the circus ring is a mere forty-two feet! The most celebrated polar bear troupe of today is Ursula Bottcher's from the State Circus of East Germany. The enormous size of these animals is made to look even more impressive beside the attractive Miss Bottcher, who nonchalantly kisses her charges and feeds them meat by hand.

Further spectacle can be introduced to the big cage by mixing different species of animals together. At the turn of the century, Frank C. Bostock, dubbed 'The Animal King', toured his 'Jungle Arena' shows around the world, playing at New York's Coney Island, the Paris Hippodrome and Earl's Court in London. He was a member of the English Bostock family, famous for their continuance of the menageries begun by George Wombwell in 1805. At the height of Frank C. Bostock's career, he was said to have had 1000 animals in various shows. Virtually the entire performance consisted of trained wild animals. When it opened at the Paris Hippodrome in 1903, as well as separate groups of polar bears, tigers, leopards and lions, there was a mixed group presented by Herman Weedon including two lionesses, tiger, leopard, puma, two striped hyenas, polar bear, brown bear and two white mastiffs. In the 1920s and 1930s, the Frenchman Alfred Court took the mixing of wild animals to its ultimate, and he trained presenters to show each of the acts he produced. When the Second World War broke out, he gathered together from various circuses in Europe his six trainers and nearly 100 wild animals to sail to America where he stayed until his retirement to the South of France, dying there in 1977. Court's group of eight lions, three polar bears, two black bears, two leopards, two tigers and a jaguar was a sensation at Blackpool Tower Circus in the 1930s. The close proximity of the audience to the eighteen wild animals in this intimate building was superbly effective. At Court's command, the animals sat up in the darkened cage, illuminated only by great shafts of light from below coming from bulbs in the pedestals.

In the big cage of today's circuses, the natural power and grace of the tiger, the leopard and the lion can be displayed in a way that visitors to a zoo or safari park seldom see. Appreciation of the beauty of a jumping tiger or the speed of a leopard suggests that there is perhaps an educational role for the circus which it is not yet exploiting to the full; and the close relationship between trainer and animal gives rise to a fascinating interaction which could usefully be the subject of scientific study.

Right: *Charismatic star of the Ringling Circus, Gunther Gebel-Williams, is a particularly fine animal trainer. Here he is seen with Prince, a magnificent Bengal tiger, riding on the back of Konga, his remarkable African elephant. Also in the Ringling show, he presents a herd of Indian and African elephants, liberty horses and, in the big cage, a group of nineteen enormous tigers and his group of leopards, black panthers and pumas.*

ACROBATS, BALANCERS & JUGGLERS

A great many circus acts are showcases for physical ability and dexterity that is out of the ordinary. Performers on the trapeze and the wire will be looked at in a later chapter, *In the air*, but there are many circus acrobatic numbers which take place at ground level.

Large troupes of acrobats belonging to one family were to be found in most circuses at the turn of the century. Apprenticeship for the youngsters was hard. Frank Foster, the famous ringmaster of Bertram Mills' Circus, recalled in his book *Pink Coat, Spangles and Sawdust* that his mentor, strongman/juggler Martialo, used to remind him every morning to 'practise when you can, work when you cannot practise and sleep when you can neither practise nor work'. Coco the clown's apprenticeship to the famous Truzzi circus in Russia resulted in him being a competent rider, acrobat, juggler, trapeze artist and funny man at the tender age of thirteen.

Only perfection was good enough. Work was plentiful, with the permanent and touring circuses in Europe, three rings to be filled in the circuses of America and numerous music halls and vaudeville theatres. Many of these families were sadly broken up by the First World War, which also saw an end to many of the permanent circus buildings. During long engagements at such venues, the acts could take advantage of lots of practice time. Whereas horse and wild animal trainers, and clowns, tended to stay with a particular circus for many years, acrobatic acts were forever on the move from show to show and they were often able to boast in their old age of having travelled the world. The Craggs, a famous English act popular late last century, worked in America, India, China, Egypt and Australia as well as Europe.

There was greatly renewed interest in circus acrobatics after the Second World War caused by the appearance outside Russia of the Moscow State Circus in the 1950s. The Russian acrobats have to reach a high standard of technical skill and artistic presentation before they can appear in public. Artistes are trained in special schools throughout the Eastern bloc and many acts appear in Western Europe and America. Most big troupes of today are made up of graduates from these schools rather than members of one large family as in previous years. These acrobatic acts from Eastern Europe are once again enabling circus directors to balance their programmes more evenly with equine, wild animal, clown and acrobatic numbers.

Chinese acrobats are today upholding a tradition dating back 2,000 years. There are said to be over 50,000 acrobats in China now and their recent visits to the west have shown that, like the Russians, their routines are novel and of a high standard. *The Dance of the Lions*, seen in the Chinese Acrobatic Theatre from Shanghai, is based on a folk tale. In it, a boy and a girl acrobat tease two 'lions', each acted by two acrobats wearing red and gold costumes with large stylized lions' heads. The Chinese acrobats' performances also give audiences a chance to enjoy their skills with diabolos, spinning plates and in cycling and contortion work.

Acrobats work well into their sixties and some say they are in their prime at fifty. British acrobat, Johnny Hutch, claimed to be at his peak at the age of sixty-six when he still performed the Tinska Tigenna – Arabic for a 'Roundo flip-flap' or full twisting back somersault. Johnny has two very successful routines which his troupe perform. As the Herculeans, they are a troupe of old-time acrobats dressed in leotards and complete with Kaiser moustaches. As the Halfwits, the troupe dress up as crazy characters – from Groucho Marx to Superman – and vault at speed over a gym horse, with Johnny himself as a little old lady with a feathered hat and black dress.

Left: *German Bob Bramson is a hoop juggler of extraordinary dexterity and control. Assisted by his mother for many years before her retirement, he is now partnered by his attractive Hungarian wife, Liz. Bob Bramson is seen here in action at the 1977 Circus World Championships.*

Left: *Plate spinning is a traditional art demonstrated here by the Chinese Acrobatic Theatre of Shanghai. In recent years, Western performers have produced a variation on the plate spinning act, by having their plates revolving on fixed stands. Although many have copied his act, few have made it as entertaining as the originator, Bartschelly.*

At the age of seventy, in spite of not working professionally for many years, Abu Hamid was still able to tumble. Hamid was a Moroccan who formerly had an acrobatic act. He owned the Hamid-Morton Circus in America and bought the Steel Pier Atlantic City entertainment complex for 2½ million dollars.

Many acrobatic acts require great strength as well as skill. The traditional strong men are in short supply nowadays. Though small of stature, Englishman Tony Carrol has an impressive strong man act as 'Ivan Karl'. He was runner-up to his fellow countryman, Trevor Barnet, who, as Samson, became Circus World Champion strong man in 1977. Their contemporary, Marcus, carries on the tradition of Cinquevalli by juggling cannon balls. This superbly built German lets his audience know how heavy his cannon balls and shells are by tossing them into a large steel box. Cinquevalli, a great showman of the Victorian era, demonstrated the weight of one of his cannon balls by having it dropped 40 feet to demolish a table. He then allowed the same 48-lb ball to be dropped from the same height and he caught it on the back of his neck.

Some of the strongest men in the circus today are to be seen supporting perches, either on their shoulders or from a support around their waists or balanced on the forehead. A good

Above: *Johnny Hutch's Herculeans are seen in action here at the Circus World Championships in 1976, at which they won the Ground Acrobatics title. Veteran acrobat Johnny Hutch has been in show business for over 50 years. He made his debut in 1927 at the Empire Theatre, Middlesbrough, with the 7 Royal Hindustanies.*

51

Left: *Amazing power and control is demonstrated by the Yong Brothers, seen here as the centre-piece of the water finale of the 1978 Blackpool Tower Circus. These two equilibrists are the sons of a German-Chinese couple who retired in America in 1955. As is so often the case, the main ambition of the new generation was to follow in their parents' footsteps and to equal the quality of their work — something the Yongs have certainly done as they have been featured in top engagements all over the world, in cabaret in Las Vegas, with Ringlings, with Circus Knie in Switzerland, with Circus Barum in Germany and on tour in the Soviet Union.*

Right: *The Boitchanovi Troupe, from Bulgaria, is one of the world's best springboard acts. Here they are performing a back somersault to a human pyramid four men high at Billy Smart's Circus in Windsor. There are thirteen men and just one woman in the Boitchanovi Troupe, which is probably the world's largest group of acrobats. Most smaller springboard troupes have only one 'top mounter' but the Boitchanovis have at least three members capable of this role, including one who performs a triple somersault to three men high. In 1978, they won a Silver Clown award at the Monte Carlo Circus Festival and became Circus World Champions on the springboard.*

example of the latter is the act of the Duo Dobritch. The bearer, with his partner atop a high steel pole balanced on his forehead, climbs, monkey fashion, a pole that is fixed in the middle of the ring. In Russian circuses, the Abakaro troupe, from the Dagestan Republic, includes an artiste who walks across a high wire while balancing a perch on his forehead – with a girl at the top of the perch. Even more dangerous can be the fixed swaying poles of such daredevils as the Nocks, the Bauers or the Swaying Stars (Jimmy Fossett family), which must sadly be recorded as probably the most accident prone type of circus act. The Swaying Stars tragically lost a 16-year-old member of their family when he lost his grip during his spectacular head first slide down a 60-foot pole. Another recent fatal accident occurred as René Bugler replaced his sister in a daring cross-over trick from one high resilient steel pole to another, when the pole he reached snapped plunging him to the arena floor. Strength is also a prerequisite of the elegant human pyramids built in slow motion in an act known as *poses plastiques*, where the performers cover their bodies with gold or silver paint. This has been seen to its best effect in the Blackpool Tower Circus water finale, or at the Brighton Centre Circus in 1978 when the Trio Hyliade worked with two high ornamental fountains in the background. Such a display is in direct contrast to the high speed tumbling and pyramid building of the traditional Arab acrobats whose displays are equally effective in the modern circus.

Several acrobatic acts employ props to extend the range of their gymnastic activities. The most spectacular of these is the springboard which has traditionally been the speciality of the Eastern European countries, especially Hungary. Springboard acts have been popular since the turn of the century, bringing a great deal of excitement to the ring as the older, heavier members of the troupe propel the lighter ones through the air by dropping on to the end of a springboard, known in America as a teeter-board. Diminutive Alexander Larenty, for twenty-two years a member of the Great Magyar Troupe, was the first person to accomplish a somersault to a pyramid four men high while carrying a girl on his shoulders, in America in 1936. Larenty, now aged sixty-eight, started springboard work in his home town in Hungary when he was nine years old and was a 'top mounter' until his son took over from him. In recent years, the accepted final trick for a springboard act – a somersault to four men high – has been surpassed. The star of the 14-strong Boitchanovi troupe is a mere 13-year-old Bulgarian, Valentin Raen, who performs a backward somersault to a human column five men high. Other troupes, including several on the Ringling circuses in America, have presented a somersault to a pyramid six men high, though the human tower is supported by a steel perch pole which must give it more stability to withstand the shock when the 'top mounter' lands. The Blue Unit of the Ringling show even had a seven men high trick featured in 1979, or rather six and a half, since one of the members of the column was the troupe leader's little daughter.

Trampoline acts often take in an element of comedy for there is always the association with bouncing on a bed. The production of trampolines by American George Nissen in 1936

gave rise to a great number of such acts and a continuing record of achievement on them. In 1979, Marco Canestrelli performed an astounding septuple twisting back somersault. In other words, in the course of a back somersault off the trampoline, he twisted himself round *seven times* before landing. American Larry Griswold produced an hilarious act around a diving board set up by a miniature trampoline and, unlike many circus acts which are not able to be copyrighted, Griswold successfully hired his routine to a number of other performers.

Walking on a huge rolling globe is an ancient art seen at its most spectacular in the 1890s when artistes like Ethardo manipulated their globes up and down a high spiral track. Since the three Rogge sisters re-popularised the act for the larger circuses in the 1950s, there have been à number of globe acts in which attractive female performers walk their globes up three ramps. These often have a tense and dramatic air to them but the Anglo-Dutch trio, the Salvadors, have produced a light-hearted comedy version, in which disaster seems ever present as the girls come dangerously close to falling off their globes.

Two of the Rogge sisters are now well known solo performers. They both still feature globes in their acts. Strong woman, Miss Atlas, balances a giant globe on her forehead and her sister, the glamorous Rogana, juggles hoops on a globe. The climax of Rogana's act is her climb up a vertical ladder while balancing a sword on the point of a dagger, the end of which is held in her mouth.

Cycling acts have been part of the circus scene for over 100 years. The first bicycles were ideal for trick cycling because of their direct drive to the back wheel. Perhaps because of their small size, Japanese and Chinese excel at trick cycling. Lilly Yokoi, a Japanese-American married to a Swedish hand balancer, has astounded and charmed circus audiences with tricks on her golden bicycle. Lilly is the fifth generation of a cycling family and must be the finest trick cyclist ever to be seen in the ring. Towards the end of the act, she embarks upon a series of boomerang spins, balancing by her hands on the handlebars and spinning round 180 degrees while the bicycle is stationary.

Above: *These young acrobats are pupils of the Circus School operated by Sylvia Monfort and Alexis Gruss in the heart of Paris. Their routine, seen here in the Cirque Gruss 'à l'ancienne', or 'old-time circus', involves trampoline and 'casting' tricks, in which the 'casters', on the high platforms, catch the acrobats flying up from the trampoline. The Cirque Gruss programme stresses the versatility of Alexis Gruss, his family and pupils, who, between them, can perform over 30 different acts.*

Above: *The Bertinis are one of the most colourful and fast-moving of all cycling acts. Originally from Czechoslovakia, they are seen here at the 1976 Circus World Championships at which they won the Trick Cycling category. The climax of their act is when one girl somersaults from a springboard on to the shoulders of another who is riding a unicycle. Boards are always put down in the ring for cycling acts, to give the artistes a smooth surface to work on. Jugglers also work on boards as an uneven ring could adversely affect their timing.*

Left: *The Hassani troupe present an exciting mixture of human pyramid building and Arab tumbling. Leader Ali Hassani is married to Tamara, daughter of Coco the Clown, a former aerial and trampoline acrobat. They now have two Arab tumbling troupes, which, unusually, include their two young daughters. In December 1979 they launched their own Circus Hassani in England.*

Below: *Petite Lilly Yokoi has delighted audiences all over the world with her unbelievable agility and control on her Golden Bicycle, covered in 18 carat gold. Lilly was born in New York where her Japanese parents were engaged there with their cycling act.*

Left: *Bulgarian artistes, the Duo Dobritch hold the audience spellbound with their astounding perch pole presentation at a Gala show at the Cirque d'Hiver in Paris. Alexandro Dobritch is the leader of a troupe which presents two other first-class acts – on the Russian swing and on the trampoline.*

Below: *Attractive contortioniste Fatima Zohra brings a grace and charm to her (supposedly) painful and unlikely exercises. Inevitably a static type of act, the contortionist can nevertheless be effectively presented in the intimate European-style one-ring circuses, though they would be lost in the three-ring shows beloved of the USA and Mexico.*

The art of juggling can be traced back to ancient Greek paintings and a small statue of a juggler found at Thèbes. Juggling probably requires more dedication and practice than any other circus art. Rastelli, the greatest of all jugglers, practised for nine hours a day and his record of 10 balls being juggled at the same time still stands today, although the Russian, Ignatov, has juggled 11 rings and is now attempting 13. Juggling is seen to best advantage in the one ring circuses of Europe as opposed to the big tent and arena shows of America. Today's top jugglers, such as Kris Kremo of Switzerland, Rudy Cardenas of Mexico or the Spaniard El Gran Picaso, who juggles table tennis balls from his mouth, work in theatres and night club cabarets as well as the circus.

The great Enrico Rastelli, an Italian, was born into a family of jugglers. He out-juggled his father when a teenager and learnt the art of catching a ball on a stick held in his mouth from an oriental troupe in a circus in Russia during the time of the First World War. He was a sensation in the 1920s in Europe and America with a breathtaking act – it was said that it took an audience fifteen minutes to appreciate Rastelli's genius. He died in 1932 at the age of thirty-four and his sporting dress of white shirt, shorts, socks and plimsoles, and style of presentation were to be copied by many other jugglers.

Juggling a variety of objects requires special skills and is unfortunately seldom seen today. It is more difficult to cope with the different shapes and weights involved than in juggling clubs, hoops or balls. Michael Kara, the 'Gentleman Juggler' who worked in morning dress, juggled umbrellas, walking sticks, and gloves, and Cinquevalli juggled with an egg, a bottle and a scrap of paper. Juggling troupes at the turn of the

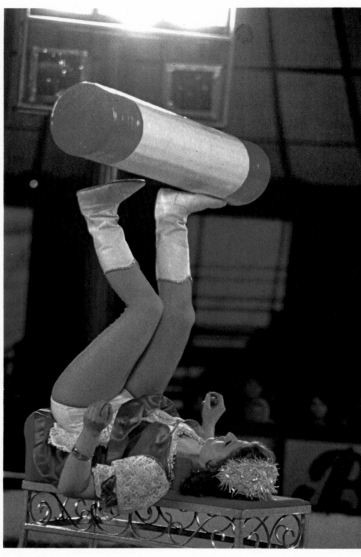

Above: Footjuggler Maureen Roberts is a member of the versatile Roberts circus family. Her father, Bobby, is an animal trainer and formerly was an acrobat on the horizontal bars with his brother, Tommy. Her mother, Kitty, trained and presented the dogs and her brothers, Bobby and Tommy, present the elephants, horses and ponies. Maureen is married to Lazlo Endresz, a member of the Hungarian circus family, the Schlingloffs. Lazlo's grandmother ran the Circus Alhambra until Hungarian circuses were nationalised in 1949.

Right: *There are ten members of the Santus troupe of jugglers, whose act is seen here on Gerry Cottle's Circus. When the family came to England from France in 1969, there were just two brothers and one sister in the act. Now the younger brothers have joined the troupe and the older ones have married so the act is ten strong. As well as the juggling routine, the Santus family are expert trick cyclists and comedy acrobats and have an act involving rolling globes.*

century, like Kara, appeared in formal dress and worked their routines to themes, such as juggling in a kitchen with plates and pans, and juggling in a hat shop with hats and hat boxes. In the early 1950s, Eric van Arno juggled with a music stand, a drum and a cymbal. Van Arno, married to Catherina Valente, also presented the novelty first shown by Everhart late last century – that of rolling hoops in patterns on the floor. The German, Bob Bramson, does the act today with a fine sense of showmanship and skill. Two comedy jugglers – W. C. Fields and Eddie Cantor – later made a name for themselves on the cinema screen. W. C. Fields juggled with cigar boxes, while dressed as an American hobo, and Eddie Cantor was in a two-man juggling act in which he was a black bell boy.

Further variety can be brought to this skill by juggling with the feet. Footjugglers are known as antipodists, since they lie on

their backs on a trinka and manipulate objects of surprising size, such as a kitchen table. More spectacular routines are possible when the footjuggler juggles people. As early as 1777, such an act was seen in Astley's performed by a Signor Colpi. Nowadays, these acts are known as Risley numbers after Professor Risley who had a popular act in the 1880s, juggling his two boys on his feet. Today, Risley acts, such as those of the stylish French brothers, Les Castor, and the amazingly athletic Rios, are amongst the most satisfying to be seen in the circus.

Juggling can be learnt but the great jugglers have a natural talent. Cinquevalli, for example, in his schooldays was said to have been able to throw a slate and piece of chalk high into the air, catch the chalk and with three lightning strokes draw the letter A on the slate as it passed him!

THE ELEPHANTS

The elephant, probably the most popular of all the animals in the circus, became quite common in the menageries of the late eighteenth and early nineteenth centuries. An 1820 poster for Wombwell's collection mentions 'that stupendous animal, the male elephant, with fine ivory tusks . . . he will lie down and rise up at the word of command . . . he will unbolt a door, and by the command of his keeper, will perform so many wonderful tricks'. There was an elephant in the circus ring at Astley's in 1827 and, by the latter half of the last century, their place of importance in the circus was well and truly established.

Elephants, the world's largest land mammals, are remarkably intelligent. They can also be temperamental and often become terrified of tiny animals, such as rats and mice. It has been suggested they are frightened of them running up their trunks. Oscar Fischer confirms this with a story of what happened on a Swedish circus. 'I had just given the word of command for my beasts to balance on their front legs on small strong white pillars when a rat ran across the ring,' he writes. 'The next moment I was surrounded with a rioting, bellowing mass of frightened elephants and it took me nearly a day to calm them down.'

Do elephants ever forget? Here again a circus story makes interesting reading. Modoc, a 78-year-old elephant on the Ringling Brothers and Barnum & Bailey Circus, let out a squeal of recognition when her former trainer, Fabian Redwood, visited her after a parting of 52 years. On Redwood's instructions, Modoc reared up on her hind legs and flung her trunk high above her head, then ambled up to Redwood, encircled him with her trunk and hoisted him level with her eyes so that she could gaze into the face which she had not seen for over half a century.

Modoc, like most elephants in the circus, was a female Indian elephant. Bulls are more temperamental and can become difficult to handle. Many came as youngsters from India, Burma, Sri Lanka and Siam, where elephants have been used for centuries as working animals in the timber forests. Because of this tradition of domestication, the Indian elephant was thought for many years to be far easier to train than the African, which has larger ears. Recently, more Africans have been seen in the circus, on Circus Knie, Circus Krone, Circus Althoff in Europe and in America where the Ringling shows have several. In England, Mary Chipperfield now has a dozen trained African elephants and finds them as easy to train as the Indian.

Left: *Mary, Janie, Ann, Maureen, Rebecca and Beverley are six teenage Indian elephants from Britain's Robert Brothers' Circus. Presented by Bobby Roberts Junior, the act is notable for the speed at which the elephants work in unison and the great control which Bobby has over his hefty charges.*

Right: *The animals are a valued and vital part of the circus. To ensure they are kept in tip-top condition, Austen Brothers' Circus in England retains David Taylor, an expert in exotic animal care, as its Consultant Veterinary Surgeon. When it comes to inspecting an animal as big as an elephant, what sort of problems are involved? David Taylor (pictured here) writes, 'Very often in zoos, this can be a considerable problem as the animals are not used to being handled. In the circus, on the other hand, the elephants are used to being close to people. They will lie down on command or lift up one leg if I need to inspect it. This makes a physical examination a much more relaxed event for elephant and vet alike!' Circuses, like Austen Brothers, which are members of the Association of Circus Proprietors of Great Britain, have a self-imposed code of standards of animal welfare and health.*

Above: *Elephant rides are a popular attraction on Circus Knie in Switzerland, a scene reminiscent of the days of Jumbo and his successors who gave similar rides until comparatively* recently at London Zoo. In 1973, over one million people visited the Knie circus and half a million went to its zoo. Morning training sessions are held in the big top and visitors can watch.

Above: *One of the reasons why Norman Barrett is such a successful ringmaster (see page 13) is that he is an all-round circus artiste. While with Bertram Mills' Circus, he became a horse* trainer and, in 1978, he presented Mary Chipperfield's African elephants at the Blackpool Tower Circus.

Jumbo, the most celebrated pachyderm of all time, was a male African elephant. The word 'jumbo', given to elephants in general and also to all things large, including jet airliners, came into popular use with the furore created when P. T. Barnum bought Jumbo the elephant for his circus in America from the London Zoo. The young Jumbo, London Zoo's first African elephant, was brought to England in 1865 from the zoo in the *Jardin des Plantes* in Paris in exchange for an Indian rhinoceros. He was then five feet six inches high. Jumbo proved to be a great favourite at the zoo, giving rides to children. All went well until, in 1881, he became difficult to handle and the zoo authorities were afraid that one day he might kill someone. As Jumbo had reached 11 feet four inches in height and weighed six and a half tons, the problem was not a small one! Agreement was reached with Barnum over the sale of the elephant but, on 25 January 1882, *The Times* announced that 'the children's favourite elephant' was to be sold. There was great concern, especially as the offer had come from – of all people – an American showman. The newspapers were full of letters from pleading children and adults. The cartoonists had a field day, music hall songs were written about Jumbo and the sale of this national institution to *The Greatest Show on Earth* gave Barnum the most fantastic publicity. The matter even came up before Parliament. Further anguish was felt when the giant animal refused initially to enter the special box made for his transportation and then pulled the hair of one of the horses which were to pull the wheeled crate, causing the team to bolt. Eventually, Jumbo sailed on the *Assyrian Monarch* on 25 March 1882 and, for three glorious years, Americans could see the mighty elephant at Barnum's Circus. Then, sadly, Jumbo was killed by a train as he was led from the ground at St. Thomas, Ontario, Canada, to the circus carriages. His skeleton stands in the American Museum of Natural History as a monument to the circus world's most famous animal.

Originally, one or two elephants only would be shown in the circus ring but in the 1870s, larger groups began to be featured. John Cooper showed six elephants on Myers Circus around this time. Elephants were a great attraction in the street parades and the importance of the circus was judged on the number of elephants carried. 'Here come the elephants – count 'em,' became a familiar cry. The Ringling show regularly contained 50 in the Thirties, Forties and Fifties and the record of 60 elephants was featured on a combined Adam Forepaugh and Barnum enterprise.

In the circus itself, the elephants are the largest and most spectacular display. The bigger shows often include girls riding on the animals and make the act into a production number with a theme. In 1979, the Ringling Blue Unit had an Oriental style elephant act presented by Buckles and Barbara Woodcock and the Red Unit had a gypsy theme for Gunther Gebel-Williams's elephant number. The ultimate in elephant production acts was surely presented by Ringlings in 1941 when they had a ballet choreographed by George Balanchine with music written by Igor Stravinsky, the concept of circus showman John Ringling North.

The bulk and slow pace of the elephant would at first seem to limit its performing ability, but this is not so as they have a good sense of balance and can work as a team. They also respond to audience appreciation. Some elephants have such an acute sense of balance that they have been taught to walk along a series of giant bottles, to roll a barrel or even walk on a rolling globe. There have been elephants who walk on thick double tight ropes. Such a feat demands that the animal must have enormous trust in the trainer, for elephants are usually

Above: *These dazzling spangled covers combine with the ponderous might of the elephant to produce the Ringling Circus Red Unit spectacle, 'Circus Toyland'. This traditional close to the first half of each Ringling show brings together hundreds of artistes, horses, elephants and other animals, and even children from the audience, who ride on the 'Teddy Bear Express'.*

extremely wary about putting their weight on anything which feels at all insecure. They sometimes work at speed, as seen in Bobby Roberts Junior's act, which is in great demand all over Europe and has twice been performed before Her Majesty the Queen. Some elephants have even been taught to play cricket and gigantic musical instruments but such acts can have the effect of making the animals look ridiculous, which should not be the aim of the circus performance at all.

Displays in which humans and elephants combine in acrobatic exercises are far more satisfying for then the element of teamwork between man and animal is paramount. At its most simple, this can take the form of a traditional circus number known as 'The Leaps' in which the forerunners of Evil Knieval leapt over lines of elephants from a running board, often turning somersaults before they landed. This has recently been seen again on Circus Knie in Switzerland and on the Ringling Red Unit where the final leaper is dressed as Superman. The act of the Hungarian Richter family is more complex. While an elephant balances on one leg, a man performs a handstand on its head. And in a spectacular springboard sequence, the elephant rears on its hind legs to bring its front feet crashing down on to the end of the see-saw, sending the acrobat at the other end into the air to land on the back of a second elephant. Louis and Franco Knie and circus superstar Gunther Gebel-Williams have also successfully brought springboard tricks like this into their elephant performances.

Elephants often work with other animals in the circus. Mary Chipperfield has a delightful 'Big and Little' routine with two big elephants and two Shire cart horses and two little elephants and two ponies. For Circus Knie in Switzerland, Louis Knie produced an act with three elephants and three tigers. In the wild, the two species would be natural enemies but Louis Knie had the tigers leaping from elephant to elephant and then each one riding a pachyderm around the ring. Such an act is only possible after lengthy and patient training. Five out of the six animals were in fact bred by the circus – it is common for tigers to breed well in captivity but it is still quite exceptional for elephants to do so. However, Circus Knie's elephants produced Sahib, a bull, in 1963, and Madura, a cow elephant, in 1965, both born at the circus winter quarters in Rapperswil. The elephants and young tigers got used to each other by being stabled reasonably close together. The elephants were trained to carry mounts by using boxer dogs as riders and then, slowly but surely, the tigers were introduced to the elephants and the routine was developed.

On the big Ringling circuses in America, the elephant is used several times in the show. As well as their own act, they appear in the opening parade and in the big spectacle which brings the first half of the show to a close. In this they are sumptuously costumed with large, colourful, sparkling blankets, which cost up to 14,000 dollars each. On tenting shows in America, the elephants are sometimes called upon to help put up the big top and to move waggons that are stuck in the mud. Of all their various roles, they are perhaps most effective in the street parade, for there can be no more certain way of telling everyone that the circus is in town!

Left: *Louis Knie presented his amazing routine involving three tigers and three elephants in 1975 on Circus Knie. Louis' father, Rolf Knie, was also a celebrated elephant trainer – the herd of African elephants in Basle Zoo was trained by him.*

Louis' wife, Germaine, comes from the Theron family, whose 'New Dollys' cycling act is glamorous, sophisticated and skilful.

Above: *These young Indian elephants are trained and presented by Carlos MacManus on Britain's Gerry Cottle Circus. Carlos, a former rider, clown and rope spinner, had the honour of presenting his elephants at a special Royal*

Gala show in front of the King of Sweden. Since the export of elephants from the wild is now under strict governmental control, there are several moves in Europe and America to set up breeding groups of elephants to attempt to safeguard its future.

IN THE AIR

Some of the most exciting and spectacular circus performances take place not in the ring itself but above it. Although there are many types of aerial act, they can broadly be put into two categories – those involving acrobatics on a rope or wire, and those using a trapeze.

The history of rope walkers dates back to ancient Greece and Rome, the French word *funambule* coming from the Latin *funis*, meaning rope, and *ambulare*, meaning walk. There are many instances of funambulists performing at fairs and celebrations during the Middle Ages and it was not surprising that a rope walker was among the first of the acrobats that Astley added to his shows in London at the end of the eighteenth century.

As performers became more daring, they planned more and more elaborate ways of demonstrating their skill and courage, and, without doubt, the most sensational was that conceived by the Frenchman Jean Francois Gravelet, who became world famous as Blondin, the man who crossed the Niagara Falls on a tight rope. His first crossing took place on 30 June 1859 and it took him 8 minutes to walk the thousand feet between the American and Canadian borders. Blondin's achievement attracted publicity but his feat was so incredible that it backfired when people began to allege that the whole story had been invented by local hoteliers who wanted to attract tourists to the area. So Blondin returned to the Falls and walked across them again. In all, he made crossings on four different occasions. Sometimes he walked across blindfolded. He crossed while pushing a wheelbarrow. He even took passengers pick-a-back at £5 a time. Blondin's fame was considerable and, when he came to England in 1862, people flocked to the Crystal Palace to see 'The Hero of Niagara'. He cleverly included some new feat at each show. He would carry his little daughter on his shoulders and sometimes even cooked an omelette on a huge stove on the rope. The publicity for each new feature ensured a growing audience for Blondin and people who had seen him once came back repeatedly as his repertoire changed. In 1875, Blondin walked a rope between two masts of the P & O steamer *Poonah* in high seas. Several people fainted when the swell caused him to sit down but Blondin never lost his nerve. In 1884, in Florence, he crossed the river Arno to raise money to help the sufferers from cholera in that city. In spite of the dangerous nature of his calling, Blondin continued working until he was seventy and died in retirement in 1898.

Left: *Marguerite Michelle is an astounding aerial artiste who hangs suspended by her hair on the Ringling Circus. As well as juggling while in this position, she also undertakes a series of gruelling mid-air spins. Hanging by the hair was originally a Chinese speciality.*

Tragically, the death of the most famous contemporary wire walker, Karl Wallenda, came in a far more violent manner, when he was swept from the high wire by a gust of wind while walking between two hotels in San Juan, Puerto Rico, on 22 March 1978. He was killed immediately after falling 120 feet to the ground. Wallenda began his career in 1921 when he joined the Original Louis Weitzmann Troupe at the age of sixteen. He was the only person Weitzmann could find who could satisfactorily perform a hair-raising handstand on Weitzmann's feet as he did a headstand on the high wire. After the Wallenda family had perfected their own act, they were spotted by John Ringling North in Cuba and this led to the Great Wallendas being featured on the Ringling Brothers and Barnum & Bailey Circus for sixteen years. The highlight of their routine was a three-high pyramid. Two men rode bicycles on the wire and a bar was carried on their shoulders, linking them together. A chair was balanced on this bar. Karl Wallenda stood on the chair and a girl stood on his shoulders. They were a sensation wherever they appeared but inevitably the danger of their routine led to accidents. During the history of the Wallendas, three members of the troupe were killed and one was paralysed but Karl himself always returned to the wire. 'The dead are gone and the show must go on,' he has often been quoted as saying. In more recent years, Wallenda became equally famous for special marathon walks. He walked a 1100-foot cable across the Tallulah Gorge in Georgia and a television film of the event, *A Walk in the Sun*, was shown all over the world. In November 1976, he walked a high wire by London's Tower Bridge to publicise the first Circus World Championships and the following year he took part in this competition with his own troupe. His appearances then were made particularly remarkable as he had broken his neck only weeks before while making a film based on his life in Florida. Wallenda was obsessed with the high wire. It seems likely he would never have retired. Asked in 1976 how much longer he would like to work, he replied, 'As long as the good Lord lets me.'

While danger is always present on the high wire, you should also be able to appreciate the artistry and skill of the performer. Where large troupes are featured, a safety net is often used. When a net is not seen, there is often someone close at hand ready to break the fall should the performer come off the wire. This happened in 1947 when Harold Alzana, an ex-miner who became one of the finest of all wire walkers, and his sister fell. Their father, Charles, was there and broke their fall. The most sensational high wire to be seen today is probably that of the Columbian Carillo brothers, on the Red Unit of the Ringling Circus. A spine-tingling routine reaches its climax as one man stands on his partner's shoulders and then jumps down to the wire. Pedro Carillo's previous partner is still recovering from a serious fall which left him paralysed, so Pedro now works with a new partner, for, like Wallenda before him, he is obsessed with his act.

Manfred Doval became the Circus World Champion on the high wire in 1976 and retained the title in 1977. He does not use a balancing pole except for the final trick when he walks the wire on stilts. Further variety can be introduced by using wires at an angle and the artistes of the Russian State Circuses are the main innovators in this area. The troupe of Vladimir Voljanski, for example, uses a series of wires, each leading higher than the last and some operated by electric motors to increase the angle. A number of the Voljanksis' tricks would be almost impossible if the performers did not wear safety lunges and there is a rather strict school of thought which suggests that such tricks are 'cheating' if they are not performed entirely free.

No one wants to be witness to a tragic accident and the majority of today's high wire artistes have carefully calculated the skill and courage required to make their work highly dangerous, though not suicidal. Occasionally someone does still accomplish the apparently impossible, just as Blondin did when he crossed the Niagara Falls. One recent such feat was by another Frenchman, Phillippe Petit, who put on the highest high wire act ever in 1974 by walking – illegally – between the

twin towers of the 1,350-foot high World Trade Center in New York. Petit and his accomplice, who had smuggled cables and equipment into the building, were charged with trespassing and disorderly conduct but the benevolent sentence passed was for Petit to stage a free show in New York's Central Park.

The low wire provides less danger from falling to the ground than the high wire but there is the ever-present possibility of missing your footing when you land after a jump or somersault and injuring yourself on the taut steel wire. Some of the most stylish performances in the circus take place on the low wire. The Australian Con Colleano was the first to perform the forward somersault feet-to-feet, in Johannesburg in 1923. This is more difficult than the backward somersault since the performer lands virtually 'blind' on the wire. With the backward, he can see the wire as he turns and adjust his landing accordingly. Before the Second World War, only a handful of artistes could accomplish the forward somersault. Now the majority of top class male wire walkers feature it. Several have mastered the back somersault through a hoop and one, Luis Munoz, can perform a 'layout' back somersault – that is, his body remains straight, not tucked, throughout. Munoz, a prize winner at the Monte Carlo Circus Festival, has also accomplished the double somersault on the wire during practice sessions – but not yet in public. In December 1978, Munoz was contracted to appear in the touring version of the Monte Carlo Festival in America and so he was unable to appear at the third Circus World Championships. His cousin, Jose Luis Munoz, replaced him and won the Tight Wire title with a display of great skill and style. He used two wires, one considerably higher than the other, performing the forward somersault on the low wire and the backward through a hoop on the high one.

Female low wire artistes rarely include somersaults but the routines of Mimi Paolo and the Hungarian Brenda Larenty are

Left: *Jose Luis Munoz performs the backward somersault through a hoop which helped to gain him the Circus World Champion title on the tight wire. His somersault takes place 24 feet above the ground. An acrobat of great skill and panache, Munoz usually works with his father but appeared as a solo performer for the Championships. His sister, Senorita Maty, is a first rate contortioniste.*

Right: *Manfred Doval is the only artiste to have won a Circus World Championship title for two years running. His sensational routine, working without safety net, lunge or balancing pole (except for his final trick), has taken him all over Europe and America and also to Australia, New Zealand and the Far East. Doval has practised his art from an early age. When he was fourteen, he joined the celebrated Camilla Meyer high wire troupe and toured the United States with them. He has fallen only once, in Havana, and his injuries kept him in plaster for nine months.*

Right: *The great Karl Wallenda, a legend in his own lifetime, made a guest appearance on the high wire at the first Circus World Championships in London in November 1976, before presenting the Champion's award to the winner of the High Wire category that year, Manfred Doval. Wallenda was killed in March 1978 when he fell from the wire in Puerto Rico. In recognition of his wholehearted support for the Circus World Championships, the 1978 competition was dedicated in his memory and the Championships special trophy, given occasionally for an outstanding contribution to circus, was named the Karl Wallenda award.*

particularly successful because they include a variety of dance steps – last century, Napoleon I was an earnest admirer of the tight rope dancer, Antoinette Saqui. The beautiful film, *Elvira Madigan*, is based on the true story of an army officer who deserted in order to run away with a rope walker and who subsequently shot first her and then himself. Known as the circus princess in the Madigan family circus, Elvira eloped with Count Sixten Sparre when the circus was visiting the town of Sundsvall in 1889. Her tragic story has become the basis of a well known song in Sweden. A contrast to the athletic accomplishments of the male wire walker, the ballerina on the tight wire remains one of the most delightful and romantic of all circus acts.

The rope that Fortunelly the clown balanced on at Astley's was not pulled tight but left slack, and the wobbling which results from walking on the slack rope is often exploited in comic performances. The rope has become a wire in the current acts of jugglers on the slack-wire like the Bonaccorsos and Mimo Veneziano but acrobats on a rope can still be seen today. Actually, the rope is a covering for the wire which enables the performer to bounce up and down on it while in a sitting position. Somersaults can therefore be made with a greater certainty of landing correctly, though the sight of a single or even a double somersault on the bounding rope can still be a spectacular and almost painful one.

As well as rope walkers being commonplace in the period before the appearance of the circus as we know it today, there were other open-air gymnasts who also used a single rope strung horizontally. But they swung from it rather than walking on it. Such acts have today become known as 'the cloudswing'. The rope can also be hung vertically and the acrobat – almost always a girl – climbs up it and performs various holds and contortions near the top. This type of work is known picturesquely as *la corde lisse*. In the early part of the nineteenth century, the single trapeze was also occasionally seen but it was not until 1859 that one of the most exciting and romantic forms of aerial display was seen – the flying trapeze.

The flying trapeze was the invention of the Frenchman, Léotard, whose name lives on in the one-piece costume worn by acrobats. Léotard's father had a gymnasium and swimming bath in Toulouse. One day, when he was about to go for a swim, he noticed the cords which opened and closed the ventilators in the roof. They gave him an idea – if he joined each pair together with a wooden bar, he would be able to swing out over the pool. If he fell, all he would get would be a good ducking! Léotard practised with his father and in November 1859 he made his début at the Cirque Napoleon (now the Cirque d'Hiver) in Paris. Léotard and his flying trapeze were an instant success. The following March, Léotard 'fever' moved to Berlin where he appeared at the Renz Circus. There were Léotard ties and cravats and fashionable restaurants served everything from peaches to herring *à la Léotard*. He received a deluge of love letters, medals and invitations to dinner. When he started, Léotard used two trapezes and a pair of rings but eventually he was using five trapezes in line, somersaulting from one to the other. Léotard first appeared in Paris at the age of twenty-one but sadly his success was shortlived for he died of smallpox in Spain only ten years later.

The trapeze style that Léotard developed – 'flying' from one trapeze bar to another – is still sometimes seen today (by the Zemgannos and the Leotaris, for example) but the vast majority of 'flying' acts, as they are known, involve an acrobat (the 'flyer') moving from one trapeze to be caught by another acrobat (the 'catcher') who hangs from the second trapeze. The first team to do this was probably the Spanish Rizarelli brothers

Left: *Aimée Santus is a graceful artiste on the corde lisse, a type of aerial act almost exclusively performed by women. Aimée, a member of an old established French circus family, is married* to Russell Mack, whose brothers run Circus Hoffman in Britain.

Above: *Brenda Larenty has one of the best low wire routines to be seen today. She took a shorthand and typing course before the lure of showbusiness proved too much and she followed in her mother's* footsteps first practising on a wire strung between two trees in their garden. Brenda's twelve years of ballet training was useful for her routine as 'the ballerina on the wire'.

who appeared at the Holborn Amphitheatre in London in 1870. One of the Rizarellis hung from the knees in order to catch his partner but another trapeze act employed a more intriguing method. Harry Nutkins recalls seeing the act of Arien and Ostara at Hengler's Circus in London in November 1908. The catcher in this duo hung from his trapeze bar by hooks which were fixed into the heels of his gladiator-type boots!

Flying from trapeze to catcher meant that more difficult feats were possible than in the trapeze to trapeze style. The *Guinness Book of Records* lists Lena Jordan in Sydney in April 1897 as being the first person to perform the triple somersault but probably the most stylish to perfect it was the great Alfredo Codona, a Mexican whose act was judged to be the best in the world in the 1920s. In spite of its success, the act ended in tragedy. Codona had married the star aerialist, Lilian Leitzel, whose act on the Roman rings was as famous as the Codonas'. Leitzel died in 1931 in Copenhagen when metal fatigue in her apparatus caused her to fall. Two years later, Codona married his partner, Vera Bruce, but, after straining a muscle, he started to drink. Vera Bruce asked for a divorce but, after an attempted reconciliation, Codona shot first his wife and then himself. The Flying Concellos were an equally fine troupe of the same time and Antoinette Concello also performed the fiendishly difficult triple somersault. After retiring from flying, she became aerial director for the spectacles staged by the Ringling Brothers and Barnum & Bailey Circus, a post she holds to this day.

Writing in 1947, the French circus writer, Henri Thétard, recorded that he had seen only five people perform the triple in the past forty years. Nowadays the feat is far more common, although it still retains its magic. It took Mexican Tito Gaona (of the Flying Gaonas on the Ringling Blue Unit) two years to perfect his superb triple. He says, 'The hardest part is not the three somersaults – anyone can do that. The hard part is being able to stop spinning, to think clearly enough to open up and reach for the catcher's arms at the right split second.'

One of the most famous girl circus stars of the moment, Terry Lemus, is following in the footsteps of Lena Jordan and Antoinette Concello by performing the triple somersault. Terry started working on the trapeze when she was five with her eleven-year-old sister, Kandy, at the Recreation Department in St. Petersburg, Florida. Her sisters Maureen and Marleen and brother Jimmy joined them and, as the Flying Cavarettas, they became the first teenage flying act and the only one at that time in which all the flyers were girls. Nowadays, the act spends most of its time in the Circus-Circus casino in Las Vegas, performing high above the gamblers and one-arm bandits. They have also toured extensively in Australia, New Zealand, and Manilla, and, on 28 May 1977, they appeared in Windsor at Billy Smart's Circus for a special Royal Command show in the presence of Her Majesty the Queen, who had seen them on television and particularly asked for them to be included in the show. In December 1977, they became the Circus World Champions on the trapeze at the annual Championships in London, beating their fellow Americans, the Rock-Smith Flyers, who had won the previous year. Terry Lemus and her sisters cut a sparkling picture as they accomplish difficult flying tricks with great charm and appeal. Their movements are choreographed to modern musical accompaniment and the attractiveness of the girls is matched by the handsomeness of their brother, catcher Jimmy. It is Terry's triple which sets the seal on their performance. Although she has done it thousands of times, it still requires great dedication to accomplish it. 'Before I do it, I go through the whole trick in my mind – exactly how it should be done,' she says. 'I must make sure I get over far enough for my brother to reach me and to stay in the third somersault until I feel his hands touch my arms. It takes a lot of concentration and, when I lose it, that's usually when I miss. My emotions run quite high throughout the whole thing. Before the trick, I am very nervous. I'm not afraid of getting hurt, only of failing. When I catch it, I am thrilled, relieved and very, very happy. The feeling is just as strong now as when I caught the very first one.'

It can be hard to maintain the performance of such difficult trapeze tricks, just as the athlete in competition finds it difficult to perform at a consistent level. Falls are inevitable and the safety net is always used for flying trapeze acts.

The Cavarettas lost their Circus World Championships title in December 1978 when South Africa's Flying Oslers beat them in the final of the competition. Ace flyer, Freddy Osler, whose triple somersault and subsequent double pirouette when returning to the trapeze bar is an exhilarating sight, was first introduced to the trapeze by Keith Anderson. Keith's Circus School at the YMCA in Cape Town was started to provide an athletic challenge to the city's youth, including many from

Left: *French artiste Gerard Edon has a particularly dangerous routine, balancing on his solo trapeze as it swings high above the circus ring. A Parisian, Gerard Edon was not born into a showbusiness family and he worked as an electrician before first presenting his trapeze routine in the Cirque Medrano in Montmartre. The Medrano building has, alas, now been demolished. Edon presents his dangerous manœuvres with great style. His act is enhanced by specially written music and his costumes are heavily decorated with sequins and rhinestones. Unlike flying trapeze artistes, solo trapezists, like Gerard Edon, do not usually work with a* *safety net, since they are not actually flying from trapeze to trapeze.*

Right: *One of the most exciting movements on the flying trapeze is the 'passage' or passing leap, seen here performed by the Rochelle Flyers from South Africa on Jimmy Chipperfield's Circus World. The girl flyer has previously been caught by the legs by the catcher, who now returns her to the trapeze bar as the male flyer leaves it to be caught by the catcher.*

Above: *The actual moment of 'the catch' is dramatically shown in this close-up photograph of the Flying Padillas, from Mexico, at the Circus World Championships. The force with which the flyer and catcher can meet is considerable. It was estimated that Alfredo Codona left his trapeze at a speed of 62 miles per hour in order to do his triple somersault in the space of* seven square feet. *If timing and control is not correct, both artistes can receive very nasty knocks. Several catchers have received broken jaws or had teeth knocked out by the hands – or feet – of the flyers they were endeavouring to catch. For all its grace of performance, the flying trapeze is a hard taskmaster when it comes to perfection.*

Right: *Glamour is an essential element of the circus in general and the flying trapeze in particular. While the Flying Cavarettas are unquestionably among the finest of today's flying acts technically, they are also high scorers when it comes to glamour. From right to left: catcher Jimmy Cavaretta and his sisters, Maureen, Kandy and triple somersaulter Terry. Terry* is listed in the 'Guinness Book of Records' *as the only artiste to have performed the triple somersault with one-and-a-half twists, at Circus Circus in Las Vegas in 1969.*

broken homes or 'problem families' of one sort or another. Many flying trapeze acts have come out of the school and one of the largest flying troupes ever, the 10 Star Lords, from Anderson's school, made its European circus début at the Centre Circus in Brighton in July 1978. Several acts prior to this had been double flying acts – that is using two pairs of trapezes and two catchers – but this was a triple flying act, with three catchers, and at one moment eight members of the group were in the air at once.

The dedication required to perfect the triple somersault was dramatized in the film *Trapeze* starring Burt Lancaster and Tony Curtis. *Trapeze* told the story of a young American, Tino Orsini (Tony Curtis), who had an obsession to perform the triple somersault. He was taught by Mike Ribble (Burt Lancaster) who also acted as his catcher. Tino achieved his ambition in the Cirque d'Hiver in Paris and was signed up by Ringling Brothers and Barnum & Bailey. The film was directed by Sir Carol Reed and also starred Gina Lollobrigida. Tito Gaona was inspired to keep on attempting the triple by seeing the film. More recently, the three-and-a-half somersault has been performed in which the flyer is caught by the legs. The first recorded was by Tony Steel to Lee Stath in Durango, Mexico, on 30 September 1962, according to the *Guinness Book of Records*. Don Martinez, one of the world's finest flyers, has perfected it as has his former partner's son, Gino Farfan, on the Ringling Red Unit. The most consistent performers seen by the authors were Greg Friel and Dave Smith of the Rock-Smith Flyers featured at the 1976 and 1977 Circus World Championships, who never failed on those occasions to achieve the trick. As well as the three-and-a-half, the quadruple somersault is being attempted by several trapeze artistes, though none have performed it successfully in public to our knowledge. When such a feat is perfected it will be as important in terms of achievement as Roger Bannister running the four minute mile or Bjorn Borg winning the Wimbledon tennis finals four years in succession!

It is almost always the flyer who receives the limelight, yet the role of the catcher is obviously vital. They must work together as a closely coordinated team as split second timing is essential. The flyer must also have confidence in the catcher. Horst Saltas, a catcher with his own troupe, the Flying Saltas, has described how inexperienced flyers tend to let go if they think they have not achieved a tight grip after a trick, whereas Horst can very often hold them nevertheless.

As well as the flying trapeze, there are many other types of trapeze act. The solo trapeze can be seen in almost every circus and enterprising artistes have incorporated the trapeze into more elaborate machines. The Antares, for example, have a giant rotating apparatus, powered by a miniature aeroplane driven by Patricia Antares, while her two brothers perform exacting feats suspended from a bar at the other end. Werner Bronley brought the act right into the space age with his fast-moving rocket ship, which enters amidst a great sea of dry ice to simulate the surface of the moon. Elvin Bale, trapeze star of the Ringling Circus, has also brought another traditional circus act, the Human Cannonball, bang up to date with his 'Human Space Shuttle' launching.

The aerialists of today are proving themselves to be just as thrilling as those of the last century, one of whom inspired a contemporary song writer to record, 'He flies through the air with the greatest of ease, the daring young man on the flying trapeze.'

A GREAT VARIETY OF ANIMALS

It would be unthinkable to find any major circus in the world without horses, elephants or a wild animal act (lions or tigers) but a great many other species of animals have appeared in the circus, including such popular performers as chimpanzees, dogs and sea-lions and such unlikely ones as ostriches, hippopotamuses and alligators.

Dogs have played their enthusiastic part in circuses large and small. Poodles are often seen and the act presented by Phyllis Allan is an object lesson to all aspiring trainers. Phyllis originally worked exclusively with horses and ponies on the Bertram Mills Circus where she was asked to train a poodle act. As well as appearing on the Mills show for many years, Phyllis has worked for Billy Smart's Circus in England and the Boswell Wilkie Circus in South Africa. Her dogs throw themselves into their work with such gusto that you are left in no doubt that they are enjoying it all as much as the audience. For a fast moving finish, two dogs race round the ring fence, jumping over two standard poodles as they do so. A third, smaller dog joins in the race and, not to be outdone, he saves time by running through the legs of the two standards in his efforts to win the race.

Dogs can be successfully trained to make fun of their trainer. Former Ringling clown, Eric Braune, was a big hit on France's Cirque Bouglione with his sketch enacted by his black poodle, Sloopy, and Braune as a long-suffering parksweeper. Whenever the man put some newspaper into a plastic dustbin, Sloopy would knock it over and cause Braune to trip over it. Michael Freeman has been a great success on Germany's Circus Barum with a similar act, reviving his father's 'Old Regnas' routine. 'Regnas' incidentally is 'Sanger' spelt backwards and Michael and his brother are in fact the only members of the illustrious Sanger dynasty working in circus today.

Pekinese might at first sight appear to be unsuitable as circus dogs but the Rosaires have proved them to be adept performers. Ida Rosaire, a versatile member of a famous British circus family, presented an act with pekes in variety and circus in the 1940s. She married Martin Hawkes, lion trainer on the Rosaire Circus, whose father was a country vicar in Kent. Their son, David Rosaire has shown his group of pekes in many major European circuses as well as in cabaret in Las Vegas. His act includes a cheeky little terrier, Sheeba, who becomes the

star of the show, running rings round her master in a well-conceived comedy routine. Previous generations witnessed dog acts where the animals, walking on their hind legs, were dressed up. But fashions change and today's circus dog numbers endeavour to show the animals off as dogs, not as caricature humans.

Chimpanzees are amongst the most popular of circus animals. They are both intelligent and responsive to training. Rudi Lenz is a Dutchman whose life has been devoted to chimps since the day when he and his brother (also a well known chimp trainer) took a job with Bertram Mills Circus twenty-five years ago. After thirteen years with this famous British show, he and his English wife, Sue, trained their own animals and worked in Spain and Germany before moving to the Ringling Circus in America in 1969, where they have remained a centre ring attraction ever since. Chimps are immensely strong and some become difficult to handle on reaching maturity at the age of six or seven. Nevertheless, Sue and Rudi have one chimp, Sally, now aged eighteen, who still appears in their act, although the record for longevity amongst circus chimps is probably held by Charlie of Chipperfield's Circus who was thirty years old when he died in March 1978. A temperamental star, he was a lively performer – walking on high stilts, riding a bicycle and turning back somersaults with verve.

Chimps have only been trained since around the turn of the century whereas monkeys have a far longer tradition as entertainers. Monkeys are not as spectacular as chimps for the modern circus, however, and they are seldom seen, although Mary Chipperfield has several Rhesus monkeys and baboons who, mounted on the backs of Shetland ponies, always bring the house down in their steeplechase. Apart from chimps, the other anthropoid apes – gorillas and orang-utans – have rarely been presented in the circus. A few trainers have attempted their training, among them the Berosinis in America. One of their orang-utans, Clyde, was Clint Eastwood's co-star in the film *Every Which Way But Loose.*

Although chimps and monkeys are not domestic animals, they are never presented in a cage in the circus. Rather surprisingly, bears are sometimes shown on leads, though they are usually muzzled to protect the public from their teeth. They

Left: *Here's Freddie Howes – 'Super Chimp' – in action on Gerry Cottle's Circus. Chimps have a good sense of balance and walking along a bar, especially when you can grip with your feet, is child's play to a chimpanzee.*

Freddie is part of a troupe trained and presented by Sydney Howes and his daughter, Barbara. (See page 43.)

can still do considerable damage with their claws, however, and one bear trainer had his leg broken when one of his large charges fell against him and pushed him to the ground. Bears are not affectionate in the same way as dogs or chimps but there is still a close rapport between animal and trainer. One evening when James Clubb was presenting his brown bears on Chipperfield's Circus, the generator failed and the lights went out, leaving the ring in pitch darkness. One bear immediately rushed to James and hugged him. To begin with, he thought he was being attacked but then he noticed the bear was shaking with fright and he realised she had run to her trainer for reassurance.

The potential danger involved in handling crocodiles and snakes (even of the non-poisonous varieties) has also made them intriguing to circus audiences. Reptiles cannot be trained to go through any set routine but a clever showman can produce a novel display by appearing to hypnotize them. With a dramatic flourish of the hand, he places himself in front of one of the crocodiles which stops and gazes motionless into space, to all intents and purposes under the trainer's power. Such acts rely heavily on presentation and dressing to make them more exciting. When Alham Sahari and Shira (in reality Carlos and Tina Rosaire) appeared with Italy's Orfei Circorama, they entered the ring on a barge, accompanied by exotically costumed girls, and a film of crocodiles in the wild was shown on a giant cinema screen backdrop. As well as hypnotising and displaying their reptiles, Shira entered a small square tank and swam with one, a highly dangerous act, though made less so as

Shira kept a tight grip on the crocodile's jaws. The fakir Koringa, who worked with snakes and crocodiles, was one of the great attractions in show business in the 1930s. Although she was slightly built, she was very strong and could carry her animals single handed.

Transporting and caring for a collection of crocodiles can present problems. When Karah Khavak was booked by South Africa's Boswell Wilkie Circus early in 1978, air transport from Europe was arranged for his nineteen crocodiles, alligators and caymans. Just a few days before the flight, however, Khavak discovered that the temperature in the hold dropped to below freezing at high altitudes so his animals would be frozen to death. The airline accommodatingly allowed the reptiles to travel in one of the passenger sections, with the seats removed so that their crates would fit in. Once in Johannesburg, the crocodiles were transferred to a specially built trailer with its own big tanks. At meal times, each animal was fed individually as fights would break out if they ate together, so Khavak enticed the crocodiles in turn out of the tank with the offer of a hunk of chicken on a stick. Although Karah Khavak and his wife both have scars where their charges mistook them for their dinner, they have a real affection for these giant-jawed creatures. 'My brother, he has an act with crocodiles and snakes,' says Khavak. 'Me, I don't like snakes. I prefer my crocodiles.'

Other animals who are at home in water have worked in the circus and the most popular of these is probably the sea-lion, whose appeal lies as much in his honking and never-ending appetite for fish as in his remarkable sense of balance. The

Above: *Sally Chipperfield leads her troupe of poodles into the ring at the Christmas Circus at King's Hall, Derby. Sally's dogs are joined by two Rhesus monkeys and a pony to make a 'Poodle, Pony and Monkey Revue', reviving memories of the small 'Dog and Pony' circuses once seen in America. Sally, daughter of circus director Dick Chipperfield and sister of wild animal trainer Dick Chipperfield Junior, branched out on her own* in 1978 with her husband, James Clubb, by presenting a new touring show, Sally Chipperfield's Circus. Sally met her husband when he joined Chipperfield's Circus as an apprentice wild animal trainer. Their romance blossomed as they presented alligators and pythons in an exotic Eastern act and James went on to show lions, tigers, leopards, llamas and bears.

Right: *Many European circuses travel with a menagerie, comprising the trained animals and some others, like the gorilla on the Cirque Jean Richard in France. Jean Richard is a well-known French actor who plays 'Maigret' on television. He has had a life-long interest in animals and has his own private zoo just outside Paris. His circus hobby developed from occasionally presenting groups of lions or tigers for gala shows to* owning his own circus. Now, as well as the Cirque Jean Richard, he has taken over the old established Cirque Pinder (re-named Cirque Pinder-Jean Richard) and he has presented a gigantic Ben-Hur show and the State Circuses of Hungary and East Germany in a giant Hippodrome big top in Paris.

OUI ...
DANS UN PALAIS DE VERRE
LE SEUL
GORILLE ADULTE
VEDETTE DU
ZOO
CIRQUE
JEAN RICHARD
EUROPE 1
PLACE
Mercredi
22
AOUT
Location
à 18 heures
GRANDE PARADE
JEUX-CONCOURS
LE CIRQUE
A CHOISI

Above: *American trainer Barbara Morris was able to take advantage of the sinking ring which floods with water at the Blackpool Tower Circus for her Californian sea-lions.*

Right: *A zebra on Gerry Cottle's Circus is led from its stables to the big top for the show. Most of the 'exotic' animals are kept in stables similar to those for the horses and become as used to life in the circus as they do.*

Far right: *Franz Richard Althoff presents Mary Chipperfield's llamas at the Tower Circus, Blackpool. The llama is a native of South America and is of the same zoological family as the camel, it breeds well in captivity and has been used for transporting goods in South America for many years.*

Englishman, Captain Joseph Woodward (born in 1873) discovered this and exploited it. Many sea-lion trainers since have adopted naval officer's garb, if not the actual billing of 'Captain'. Very occasionally it has been possible to present sea-lions in their natural habitat – water. Max and Barbara Morris, two fine American trainers, brought their sea-lions to the Blackpool Tower Circus in 1967 and here patrons were treated to a delightful display with the animals swiftly and gracefully gliding through the water. The act was such a success that it returned for the 1970 season. Although sometimes erroneously called 'performing seals', most acts involve sea-lions. There are

exceptions, however, and Max Morris has trained a delightful group of South African cape fur seals, which made its début at the Hippodrome Circus in Great Yarmouth in 1975. In Hagenbeck's day, even the walrus and the elephant seal made an appearance.

In the circus, camels, llamas, zebras and antelope are called 'exotic' animals, since their appearance brings a touch of the unusual to a programme. They can be trained to perform a simple liberty routine but really it is the sight of the animal in the ring which is interesting rather than what it does. Some of the most successful 'exotic' acts have been those which

introduce many different species. On Jimmy Chipperfield's Circus World, for example, Margaret Chipperfield presented a troupe of six Bactrian camels. Two of the camels were then joined by a young Highland bull and a black-and-white Tibetan yak. As the camels lay down in the centre of the ring and with the bull and the yak perched on low pedestals, a young giraffe gracefully ambled amongst them and took a titbit from its trainer. An eland and a llama demonstrated their prowess at jumping before the routine was brought to a fast climax with the appearance of a small monkey racing along on the back of a pony. In the same programme, Margaret showed a troupe of zebras and spotted ponies. Like most animals in the circus today, the zebras had been born in zoos or parks and so were accustomed to people and not difficult to train. They were common zebra but Margaret's sister, Mary, produced an act with four of the larger Grevy's zebra, which are more strikingly marked and which had probably never been trained for the circus before. Giraffes can present a transport problem as they grow older – and taller. This was neatly solved by Chipperfield's Circus who converted a double-decker bus for their pair, George and Georgina, during the 1950s and 1960s. Even so, the route from town to town had to be specially planned and large detours were sometimes taken in order to avoid low bridges.

The Swiss Circus Knie, which specialises in exotic acts, presented the unusual sight of a giraffe, Lucky, gambolling in the ring with an African white rhino, Ceyla, in 1970. In a previous production, young trainer Fredy Knie Junior had ridden the giraffe but this time the rhino was his mount. By 1972, Fredy had trained Ceyla to be ridden by a tigress and the pair made a spectacular tour of the ring, with the big cat leaping on and off the padded saddle at speed. This performance was admired by Professor Heini Hediger, former director of the Zurich Zoological Garden, who also noted that the rhino allowed itself to be led by its trainer through the roar of city traffic. Remarking upon the 'far-reaching mutual understanding' between trainer and animal, he wrote, 'Ceyla, born in the African wilds and reared among other members of its species, has, in the space of less than ten years, shown truly commendable powers of adaptation to totally different living conditions and manifested amazing open-mindedness in the face of new situations.' As man encroaches further and further into the natural habitats of wild animals throughout the world, it is inevitable that animals, if they are to survive, will often have to modify their behaviour patterns to co-exist with man. Some of the achievements of the circus provide a fascinating insight into

Right: *Through long and patient training, Circus Knie has succeeded in presenting many unusual animals. Their giraffe, seen here with Rolf Knie Junior, has its own waggon and pen on the circus. The high waggon winds down to a lower height when travelling on the railway and the interior is specially padded to protect the giraffe.*

Below: *Ceyla, the African white rhinoceros on Circus Knie.*

what can be done, given the right sort of approach.

It is not only the giants of the animal world like giraffes, rhinos and hippos that have their place in the circus ring. A variety of birds have also appeared. John Chipperfield trained the largest of all birds, the ostrich, to pull a small cart and to be ridden by a girl. His niece, Anne, presented a delicate act with pigeons and later trained a multi-coloured assortment of macaws, parrots and cockatoos, which flew freely around the big top. When she was working for Bertram Mills Circus, Sue Lenz made her bird display decidedly exotic by adding a toucan, cockatoos, macaws, Chinese geese and even a flamingo to her flock of pigeons. Probably the smallest birds to be seen in a circus are budgerigars. Norman Barrett has a delightful act with them which he presents in clubs and theatres as well as occasionally in the circus ring. There seems to be no end to the list of animals which have appeared in circus rings around the world. Many of them have been seen only briefly, for purely novelty value, rather than the performance of any tricks. Even the rare and delightful giant panda is an unexpected inclusion – the Dutch circus magazine, *De Piste*, recently published a rare archive photo of panda Weinei in a circus in Shanghai.

Left: *Juba, the hippopotamus, has been owned by the Knie circus for over 30 years. The younger members of the family grew up as she grew up. Rolf Knie Junior (seen here), the son of Fredy Knie, is a talented rider and animal trainer. He has also broken away from his family tradition by carving a career for himself as a very successful clown.*

THE CIRCUS INDUSTRY

The performance is the *raison d'être* of the circus – the occasion when all the diverse people, animals and equipment come together and produce two or three hours of exciting live entertainment quite unlike any other. But behind the colour and razzle-dazzle of the show itself there is an equally fascinating world concerned with the business organisation of the circus. Where does it play? How does it move? What is its future as we near the twenty-first century?

When Philip Astley began giving his trick riding performances in London in 1768, his shows took place in the open air. As success came his way, he built stands and later a series of buildings – Astley's Amphitheatre of Arts. Visited by the circus loving Queen Victoria and described with enthusiasm by Dickens in *The Old Curiosity Shop*, Astley's was a vital part of the social life of nineteenth-century London. It changed hands several times until sadly the great showman, 'Lord' George Sanger, was forced to give it up to the London County Council for destruction on 4 March 1893 after twenty-two years of management.

Although the Amphitheatre building was his home base, Astley also travelled with his troupes throughout the British Isles and into Europe. His pupils and rivals took the entertainment further afield. Sometimes they performed in the open air but often cheaply erected, wooden buildings were used. Where the performances proved successful, more substantial purpose-built circuses were constructed – a tradition which lasted throughout the nineteenth century and into the early years of the twentieth. There are few surviving circus buildings in Western Europe and fewer still currently in use. The Hip-

Left: *Barnie Walls, Gerry Cottle's Circus stilt-walker, proudly shows off some of the prize items in the transport fleet. After the war, many circuses eagerly snapped up the heavy duty ex-army vehicles which were ideal for adaptation to circus use.*

podrome in Great Yarmouth is one exception where Jimmy Chipperfield's Circus World played during the summer months of 1979. The famous rider, George Gilbert, opened the present building in 1903 on the site of a wooden one he had constructed in 1898. The Blackpool Tower Circus is also still thriving. This magnificently decorated circus, with gold Moorish-style decorations and red plush seats, is situated between the four legs of the Tower, 480-foot high. Opened in 1894, the Blackpool Tower was inspired by the Eiffel Tower in Paris. Other British circus buildings have disappeared altogether or are now used for different purposes. Gilbert's Circus in Lowestoft, for example, is now a bingo hall. There is no circus building in London, though Astley's was by no means the only purpose-built London circus in the past. The Hengler Circus in Argyll Street, by Oxford Circus, is now the London Palladium and the Talk of the Town theatre-restaurant in Charing Cross Road was originally built in 1900 as the Hippodrome circus by Sir Edward Moss, then chairman of the Moss Empire chain of music-halls. The circus there lasted until 1909. In Western Europe, the Cirque Royale in Brussels, the Cirque d'Hiver in Paris (opened in 1852 as the Cirque Napoleon), the Copenhagen building now used by Circus Benneweis and the modern Circus Krone-bau in Munich also still function. In Eastern Europe there are many more permanent circuses. In the USSR alone there are, according to the 1978 Intourist Guide, fifty-nine stationary circuses.

As the early circuses began performing in smaller towns and villages, away from the buildings of the cities and large towns, it was perhaps inevitable that they would begin to appear in canvas booths and, eventually, tents. The purpose-built canvas

Above: *The Cirque d'Hiver, not far from the Place de la République in Paris, is the oldest purpose-built circus building in Europe, having opened on 11 December 1852. The famous Bouglione family took it over in 1934 and its annual season runs from October to March. The Gala de la Piste, a special charity show, is often held there.*

Right: *This circus training school in Bompesta is the result of Spanish priest Father Jesus Silva's unique social experiment. He has created a 1000-strong 'Boys' Town', a democratically-run community which has produced its own, now internationally famous Circo de Los Muchachos.*

big top evolved and has since become synonymous with the circus. In spite of the great tradition of circuses appearing in buildings, there are many people who feel that the proper venue for a circus is under canvas in the open air. There are numerous aspects of the history of the circus which are not well documented – and the question of who first used a tent for his circus shows is one of them. According to historian George Speaight, Astley himself experimented in 1788 with the 'Royal Tent' for his shows in Liverpool, but the idea does not seem to have been successful as the tent was auctioned at the end of the season. Probably the first circus to tour with a tent was one in America. In an article in *Bandwagon*, journal of the Circus Historical Society, Stuart Thayer records that J. Purdy Brown was touring his circus with a tent there in 1825. By the time of the Golden Age of circuses, in the late nineteenth century, the touring big top was commonplace on both sides of the Atlantic. In Europe, there has traditionally been one act working in a single ring whereas America has delighted in the spectacular three ring circus, with three acts being performed at the

same time. Curiously enough, even this appears to have its origins in England for, in his memoirs *Seventy Years a Showman*, 'Lord' George Sanger states that he gave the first such show on the Hoe at Plymouth in 1860, with 'three circus rings and two platforms going at the same time'! It seems likely that this display organized by Sanger took place in the open air but, in America in 1872, Coup toured a show which had two rings in a tent. In 1881, Phineas T. Barnum and James A. Bailey had three rings in their touring circus, thus setting the pattern for years to come.

The big top of the one ring circus is almost always circular or nearly circular in shape, whereas tents for three ring shows have to be oval. For the former, the tiered seating needs to surround the ring, more or less in the shape of a funnel, so that the ring is the focal point for the audience and their attention is not distracted. This is less easy in the three ring set-up and it is much more difficult to concentrate on the merits of a particular act, though spectacles and big production numbers can be breathtakingly effective.

Manufacturing a circus big top is a specialised business. The German firm, Stromeyer, has established a fine reputation for making tents for many of the major European shows. More recently, plastic has been used instead of canvas and the Canobbio organization of Milan have produced dozens of big tops using this material. Plastic tents should last longer than canvas ones, which usually wear out after four to six seasons depending on treatment and weather. However, plastic big tops are heavier and more difficult to handle, as well as being expensive. One of the major European circuses paid over £30,000 for its new four pole plastic tent in 1979.

During the winter months, circuses often play in exhibition halls since the inclement weather can make tenting an unpleasant experience for artistes and audience alike. The shows in Kelvin Hall, Glasgow, Belle Vue, Manchester, the Deutschlandhalle, Berlin, are all still going strong after many years. Belle Vue celebrated its Golden Jubilee, in fact, in 1978.

However, the great Bertram Mills Circus, with its attendant fun fair, once a London institution, no longer fills Olympia's Grand Hall at Christmas time. Rising costs forced the management to play their final season in 1967.

In America, the Ringling circuses are presented exclusively in exhibition halls, having abandoned the big top in 1956 due to the difficulties in controlling such an enormous touring operation under canvas. The circus was reorganized and overheads cut drastically. It started touring the many exhibition and sports buildings which were springing up in American cities and towns at the instigation of Irvin Feld, who was to buy the entire circus from John Ringling North for eight million dollars in 1967. Feld has modernized the whole Ringling operation. He introduced the second unit in 1969 and the shows have gone from strength to strength in terms of artistic appeal and in profitability. Although some critics would say the current Ringling circuses cannot have the same atmosphere as the old outfit under canvas, no one can deny that Irvin Feld has found a way of preserving and enhancing the Ringling reputation for producing the largest and most spectacular circus in the world.

The travelling circus has often been given a highly romantic image in novels and films. In reality, moving the show entails a great deal of hard work. Many smaller circuses were using horse-drawn transport until the 1930s, augmented by steam traction engines and early petrol driven lorries. England's 'Sir' Robert Fossett's Circus, for example, like most shows of the time, used to spend one day only in each town. As Tommy Roberts, a member of the Fossett dynasty, says, 'If we stayed more than one day in a place, it was a real holiday!' The daily routine was a gruelling one. They got up at about 4 a.m. to take the horse-drawn wagons through to the next site; built up the big top and stables; took part in the free publicity parade at noon; performed several acts in the afternoon and evening shows; and then packed up the circus again ready for the early start the next morning.

The larger circuses travelled on special trains. In the early

Left: *Circus Knie has its own train for travelling in Switzerland. The circus trailers are specially built, following the pattern of almost all German and Swiss circus transport, with small wheels and low axles in order to give maximum height in the trailer. The overall height is of course restricted by the railway tunnels!*

Right: *Schooling can be a problem for circus children. Some go to boarding school or stay with relations in order to go to one school. The alternative is to attend a different school every week as the circus tour progresses. A few circuses have their own travelling school, with its resident teacher, such as Gerry Cottle's Circus (pictured here) in Britain, Circus Busch-Roland in Germany and Circus Knie.*

days of the circus in the States the coming of the railways was a real breakthrough for the American showmen. It meant that the west was opened up for big scale live entertainment, that the circuses could get more quickly and efficiently from one population centre to another and, above all, it gave the circus a modern and respectable image.

Some circuses still use railways today. The major outfits of Germany and Switzerland, staying usually two or three days in a town, move by rail and so do the Ringling Circuses in America and the Boswell-Wilkie Circus in South Africa. This latter show has been specially adapted for economical travel in a country where the big towns and cities are few and far between. Although it spends three weeks or a month in the big cities like Johannesburg or Cape Town, for much of the year it embarks on a series of one day stands. All the equipment and the lions, horses and elephants travel on the train, as do the artistes and staff, who each have their own small compartment.

The majority of today's circuses travel by road and the improved standard of roads and motorways have meant that long journeys between stands can be undertaken efficiently. Circuses in France, such as the Cirque Bouglione or Cirque Amar or Cirque Jean Richard, move every day and they have modern fleets of trucks, looked after carefully by their own team of mechanics.

In the past, several enterprising directors have taken their shows away from the usual routes in Europe and North America and embarked upon tours to Africa, Asia and South America. Probably the most energetic was Giuseppe Chiarini, born in Rome in 1823. At one time an equestrian instructor with Astley's in London, he moved to New York in 1853 and opened his own circus which was in Havana in 1856. In 1864, his show toured Mexico and he was presented with a fine Arabian horse, Ab-el-Kadar, by the Emperor of Mexico. From 1879 to 1882, Chiarini visited Australia, New Zealand, Tasmania, the East Indies and India. In 1882, command performances were given at the court of the King of Siam at Bangkok,

and, four years later, the Japanese Emperor and Empress saw his circus in Tokyo. Chiarini died in Panama at the age of seventy-four but he must have been an incredibly resilient and persevering man to have successfully transported his circus on such a remarkable series of journeys. Today's circus proprietors in Europe are on the whole content to restrict their travels to nearby countries. Italian circuses visit Yugoslavia, Greece and Israel. Jean Richard has brought the East German, Bulgarian and Hungarian circuses to France. The Moscow State Circus is regularly seen in .European capitals and also further afield in America and Australia. Britain's Gerry Cottle has taken his circus on three daring journeys in recent years. In 1976, his show was flown out to the Gulf of Oman as part of the Sultan's birthday celebrations, and it subsequently went on to Bahrain for a short season. In 1978, Gerry Cottle's Circus embarked upon two more flights – to Sharjah in the Persian Gulf and later to Reykjavik in Iceland, the first circus to appear there for nearly thirty years.

The organization required for a tour by any sizeable circus is considerable. The grounds often have to be booked a year or more in advance by a tenting circus. In America circuses are often sponsored by the local Shrine temple, a charitable organization, and appear in the local sports hall, in their own tent or in the open air. A week or so before the circus is due to appear, the advance publicity crew will arrive and alert the townspeople to the arrival of the circus by the use of posters, newspaper advertising and publicity stunts. When the show does hit town, there is often a parade of elephants, camels and horses to the ground which, although not in the same grandiose style of the parades of the last century, still helps to announce that the circus has arrived. During its stay, the show will spend large sums of money on meat for the big cats, hay for the horses and elephants and fish for the sea-lions, as well as diesel for its transport, and earth and sawdust to make the ring. Even after the show has left, the circus management has to ensure that the ground is left in good condition by removing all the litter.

Indeed, some towns in Britain demand a deposit from the circus which is only returned if the ground is left in an acceptable state.

The circus is essentially labour intensive. About 60 people travel with the larger British touring circuses, of which 20 to 30 will appear in the actual show. They could well carry over 40 animals and utilise about 60 vehicles. Compared to other forms of live entertainment, the running costs are incredibly high and rising all the time. Since the circus relies heavily on family audiences, it is difficult for the proprietor to increase his seat prices as much as his rising expenses demand. In some countries, the circus is recognized as an art form and in Russia, Hungary, Romania, East Germany and Bulgaria, the circus is run by the state with its own schools for the artistes. In East Germany, the V.E.B. Central Circus runs three circuses, Aeros, Busch and Berolina, with resident winter quarters for them all. Forty students are admitted every year to the artistes' school in Berlin for a four-year training period. In Italy and France, there are laws which recognize the value of the circus and which set aside funds that artistes or directors can apply for in cases of difficulty. In other countries, including Britain and America, there is no government help or indeed recognition for the circus, and some are finding it increasingly difficult to maintain profitability in spite of continuing public interest.

Co-operation between the circus and other business interests can be mutually beneficial. In France, the Cirque Amar has a fleet of Daf trucks and Daf advertise in the programme and are involved in publicity activities with the circus. Television commercials and newspaper advertisements often use the circus as a background for their subject. Occasionally firms have sponsored the circus but this has given rise to the smooth running of the programme being ruined by the continual interruption for commercial breaks. One European circus became a vehicle for advertising soap powder one year, with giant posters all over the big top. The experiment was not repeated the following season. In France, however, there have been several good examples of this co-operation. In Lille, the *Voix du Nord* newspaper runs its own autumn circus season and many larger French companies buy out entire circus performances for their employees and their families at Christmas to give them an *Arbres de Noel* treat.

Various attempts to bring new types of entertainment into the circus repertoire have, with a few exceptions, been failures. In the 1960s, some circuses, trying to cash in on the popularity of pop music, featured groups and singers in their shows, but the combination was not a happy one. Several promoters have put a circus and an ice show together but, since the working surfaces of each are so different, staging can be difficult, as one trainer who worked his lions on a mat on top of an ice rink will readily testify.

The most successful 'Circus on Ice' was probably that of Moira Orfei in Italy, but here two rings were used in a large tent. One ring was for the circus acts and the other was the rink for ice skating, so acts appeared in each ring in succession, producing a fast-moving show.

How the circus will adapt for the future is a vital question. Circus people are incredibly resilient and ingenious. As so much of their equipment is of a specialised nature, many now construct most of it themselves in their own workshops. The Austen Brothers Circus in England is a good example. The brothers – Brian, Michael and Patrick – are versatile performers, between them able to do a dozen different acts. They have also virtually made their own circus, including the generators, animal transporters, stables and even their own big top, 120 feet in diameter.

In promoting the circus, the most successful of today's outfits have a modern dynamic approach to their publicity, while retaining the tried and trusted traditional ingredients of the show itself. The circus, for all its appeal, must compete with a wide variety of other entertainments and activities. The Ringling Brothers and Barnum & Bailey Circus in America, under the direction of Irvin Feld, has produced a range of merchandise on the circus, ranging from T-shirts and pennants to reproductions of old posters and a splendid programme-magazine for each production. Each item serves to keep the name of the Ringling Circus in front of the public. Feld's publicity machine has also made stars out of several of the top members of his company. Gunther Gebel-Williams, the featured artiste on the Ringling Red Unit, is undoubtedly the most celebrated. He is probably as famous today as Clyde Beatty, the lion- and tiger-trainer, was in his hey-day in the 1930s and 1940. The public is interested in the stars of the circus – just as they are attracted by the stars of the theatre, cinema, television and music. In one sense, however, there are no stars in the circus, for there is little room for special treatment. Gunther Gebel-Williams, for example, is hard at work before the performances – practising, training new animals, supervising the feeding and care of his animals, washing down the elephants – before appearing with his groups of tigers, horses, leopards and elephants in the show itself.

In America, interest in the circus as an historic tradition is being fostered in several positive ways. The Circus World Museum in Baraboo, Wisconsin, is open to the public in the summer months, providing a colourful display of old-time circus parade waggons, painstakingly restored to their former glory by skilled craftsmen. There are demonstrations of unloading circus trains, using heavy Percheron horses, and there is a live circus performance. For the serious circus historian, there is a huge collection of photographs, programmes, posters and other memorabilia. The Ringling theme park, Circus World, near Orlando, Florida, is a more recent development. It, too, includes historical displays and a big circus production. In the participation circus, members of the public can try their hand at the flying trapeze or walking the wire, in complete safety, thanks to the use of special lunges and the presence of experienced instructors.

Finding suitable sites, near the centre of towns, is becoming increasingly difficult as more land is built on. In America, there are large exhibition halls in most major towns and cities, though the tenting circus is less well catered for. In several European countries, such as France, Germany, Switzerland and Italy, a site is provided in each town, often with water and electricity already available. Officialdom usually casts a benevolent eye on the circus and, in France, it is quite usual to find a large circus occupying the market square in the centre of the town, with caravans, stables and wild animal waggons in the road and tucked down side streets. The value of the circus to the community is recognised here and its visits are welcomed. This is not always the case in Britain, where ground rents are sometimes seen as a way of making a high profit from the circus. Most towns of course do recognise that the circus brings welcome entertainment to its inhabitants and it is to be hoped that, in future, all governments will give the circus the same sort of help that is extended to the theatre, opera and ballet to help it to survive.

Although the established families form the backbone of the industry, there are newcomers joining the circus every year. With this continuing intake of new blood, the business can successfully adapt and develop its ways of promotion and presentation while still retaining the traditional blend of the athletic and the exotic, the spine-tingling and the absurd, that has made the circus known throughout the world as *The Greatest Show on Earth*.

Right: *The giant German Circus Sarrasani visited South America during the worst times of inflation in Europe in 1923–5. For an outlay of £50,000 the circus sailed for Hamburg to Montevideo, with 500 artistes and staff, 400 animals, including 200 horses, 12 elephants and 20 lions. The poster was just one aspect of an advertising* *campaign tie-up with the company which supplied the trucks for the circus.*

CIRCUS CLUBS AROUND THE WORLD

The love of the circus is fostered by a network of circus fan clubs around the world. The oldest is that in America, which began in 1926. It was followed in 1934 by the Circus Fans' Association of Great Britain, founded in the ring at Bertram Mills Circus in Olympia, London. Each of the clubs and several other individuals and organizations publish magazines and newsletters about the circus. In addition, there are organized rallies to circuses, including overseas trips. The Dutch Club van Circusvrienden has gone on visits to Russia and America and the Circus Fans' Association of Great Britain ran a trip to the State Circuses of Moscow and Leningrad, for example.

Australasia
Fanfare. Newsletter of the Circus Fans' Association of Australasia. Editor: Geoff Greaves, 29 Elizabeth Parade, Charlestown 2290, New South Wales, Australia.

Belgium
Belgian Circus Fans' Club. Administration: The Secretary, Muinkkaai 6, 9000 Ghent, Belgium.

Finland
Sirkus. Newsletter published by the Tampereen Mini-Sirkus, PL 132, 33101 Tampere 10, Finland.

France
Le Cirque dans l'Univers. Magazine of the Club du Cirque. Treasurer: J. A. Marquant, 22 rue Teilhard-de-Chardin, 45100 Orleans, France.
Scenes et Pistes. Magazine published by Madame Manita Carrington, 127 rue Saint Germain, 27400 Louviers, Eure, France.

Germany
Circus Zeitung. Magazine of the Gesellschaft der Circusfreunde in Deutschland. H. D. Schweitzer, D 31, Celle, Harburger Strasse 53, Germany.
Circus Parade. Magazine of the Circus Club International. Editor: Friedel Zscharschuch, D2308, Preetz, Klesterhof 10, Germany.
Organ Showbusiness. Entertainments magazine published by Komet, Druck Verlaghaus, Klaus Endres, D-6780 Pirmasens, P.O. Box 527, Germany.
Unterhaltungskunst. Showbusiness magazine published by Henschelverlag Kunst and Gesellschaft, 104 Berlin, Oranienburger Strasse 67168, Postfach 220, DDR.

Great Britain

King Pole. Circus magazine published by the Circus Fans' Association of Great Britain. John Sheward, 9 Vicarage Road, Haydock, St. Helens, Merseyside, England.

Tober. Newsletter for circus modellers published by Circus Exhibits, 7 Church Terrace, Newbold on Stour, Stratford-upon-Avon, Warwickshire, England.

Acrobatics. Magazine celebrating the art of the acrobat published by George Garrard, 6 Elizabeth Way, Hanworth, Feltham, Middlesex TW13 7PH, England.

World's Fair. Showbusiness newspaper published by World's Fair Limited, Union Street, Oldham, Lancashire OL1 1DY, England.

Holland

De Piste. Magazine of the Club van Circusvrienden, Mevr. C. Hoorslag-ter-Kuile, Mosselkreek 6, Zwolle, Holland.

Italy

Circo. Magazine published by Egidio Palmiri, via G. Palmiri, 28, Rimini, Chiavari, Genova, Italy.

South Africa

Spotlight. Newsletter published by the Circus Fans' Club of South Africa. Secretary: Billy Victor, Box 116, Alice, Cape Province, South Africa.

Spain

Amigos del Circo. Magazine of the Spanish Circus Fans' Club. Administration: Mayor, num 4, Madrid 13, Spain.

Switzerland

Manege. Journal of the Club der Circus, Variete und Artistenfreunde, Switzerland. Editor: Reto Parolari, CVA-Sekretariat, CH-8401 Winterthur, Postfach 603, Switzerland.

U.S.A.

White Tops. Magazine of the Circus Fans' Association of America. W. B. Hohenadel, P.O. Box 375, Rochelle, Ill. 61068, USA.

Southern Sawdust. Magazine published by L. Wilson Poarch Junior, 2965 Freeman Avenue, Sarasota, Florida 33580, USA.

Bandwagon. Journal of the Circus Historical Society. Editor: Fred D. Pfening, 2515 Dorset Road, Columbus, Ohio 43221, USA.

Circus Report. Newsletter published by Don Marcks, 525 Oak Street, El Cerrito, California 94530, USA.

USSR

Sovetskaya Estrada I Tsirk. Showbusiness magazine. Available through Subscriptions Department of Collet's Holdings Limited, Denington Estate, Wellingborough, Northamptonshire.

Left: *Although a mass of publicity through posters, handbills, newspaper photographs and parades will be engendered for each visit, the circus itself is really its own best advertisement. The sight of the big top and decorative front, festooned with hundreds of tiny lights is an evocative reminder of the unique atmosphere and excitement of the circus.*

Figures in italics refer to illustrations and captions

Acknowledgements

The publishers would like to thank the following individuals and organizations for their kind permission to reproduce the photographs in this book:
All-Sport (Tony Duffy) 2–3, 6, 18, 21 below, 48, 51, 55, 70–71; Nick Birch 69; Circus Knie (Edouard Baumgarten) 84 above and below, (Foto Krenger) 4–5, 12, 16 below left, 42, 45, 85, 90–91, (Swiss Federal Railways) 57 below right; Circus World Museum of Baraboo, Wisconsin 10 above; The Cooper-Bridgeman Library 26 below; Gerry Cottle's Private Collection, photographs by Daniel Potier 85–86; The Daily Telegraph Colour Library 89, (P. Ward) 11, 50; Sandy Davidson 36–37, 93, endpapers except below left; Anne Horton endpapers below left; David Jamieson 13, 16 above, 17, 19, 20–21 above, 20 below, 22, 23, 24–25, 26 above, 30, 31 above, 34, 35, 38–39, 40, 41, 43, 44, 46–47, 52, 53, 54, 56, 58, 60–61, 62–63, 64, 66–67, 68, 73, 74, 75, 76, 77, 80, 81, 83, 88; The Mansell Collection 14–15; Daniel Potier 16 below right, 27, 31 below, 57 above and below left, 82 left; George Young Photographers 10–11 below; ZEFA Picture Library 8–9, 94–95.

Photography by Malcolm Aird 1, 28–29, 32–33, 58–59, 65, 72, 78, 82 right, 91.

The authors have used their own libraries of circus books and collections of circus programmes, posters, magazines and other memorabilia, as well as contemporary newspaper reports during the nineteenth and twentieth centuries. Certain circus books (such as classics like *A Seat at the Circus* by Antony D. Hippisley Coxe and *La Marveilleuse Histoire du Cirque* by Henri Thetard) and the *King Pole* have been of particular value.